The Wild Girls Club

The Wild Girls Club

Tales from Below the Belt

By

Anka Radakovich

Crown Publishers, Inc.
New York

To Jim Radakovich, my cool brother,
Lou Radakovich, my funny dad,
and Ann Radakovich, my best girlfriend/Mom

Portions of this book appeared in *Details* magazine
in slightly different form.

Published by Crown Publishers, Inc., 201 East 50th Street, New York, New York 10022. Member of the Crown Publishing Group.

Random House, Inc. New York, Toronto, London, Sydney, Auckland

CROWN is a trademark of Crown Publishers, Inc.
Manufactured in the United States of America
Design by Kay Shuckhart

Library of Congress Cataloging-in-Publication Data
Radakovich, Anka.
The wild girls club: tales from below the belt/by Anka Radakovich.
1. Sex–Humor. 2. Sex–Anecdotes, facetiae, satire, etc.
I. Title.
PN6231. S54R33 1994
306.7'0207–dc20   94–1196

ISBN 0-517-59631-8

10 9 8 7 6 5 4 3 2 1

First Edition

Acknowledgments

Special thanks to S. I. Newhouse, Jr., whose encouragement made this book possible. Big sloppy kisses to my *Details* supereditors, James Truman, Joe Dolce, and David Keeps. And thanks to my superagent, Jim Stein.

Contents

Facts of Life

The Wild Girls Club

The Determinator

Interviews of Men with Penises

Appendix

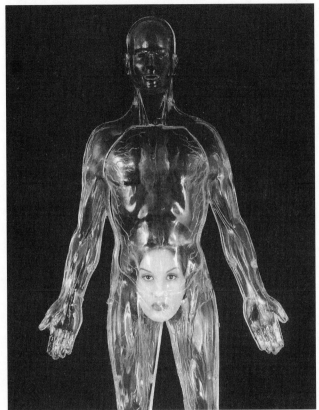

Jim Radakovich

Testosterone

Girl Talk

Tales from Below the Belt

I t's Sunday night in a loft somewhere in lower Manhattan, and ten of my supervixen girlfriends are sitting around talking—not just ordinary talk, but girl talk. It's the biannual meeting of the Wild Girls Club, and any man who tries to enter is forced to return after midnight, Chippendale's-style.

My friends, a group of sexy and smart bohemian artists, actresses, filmmakers, writers, and musicians, are here to trade top-secret information. The first thing men want to know about these parties is "What do you discuss?" Well, we always begin with discussions of semiotics, Nietzsche, and nuclear physics. Then we move into more important topics, like who's sleeping with whom and how to give a better blow job.

When men hang out, they *do* things. They shoot pool, play basketball, or watch the Super Bowl and comment on the Dallas Cowboys' cheerleaders. When women get together, we sometimes drink, often eat, and always yap. Exchanging intimacies and revealing yourself is something most men do only in rehab or group therapy.

The roots of girl talk take hold early. As soon as I could talk, I was telling my mother everything. This line of communication continues into adolescence, when prepubescent girls discover the phone. They use it and abuse it, and I was no exception. I started at an early age, and by twelve I had my own pink Princess installed in my bedroom. Back then, the main topic of conversation was boys, boys, and boys. I haven't stopped talking since, and when I can't get together with my friends, the phone is my grapevine.

What makes our gatherings different from boys' night out is that nothing is too personal to say. And nobody drinks ten beers and throws up. The only problem is that there simply isn't enough time to navigate the maze of male behavior and try to make sense out of it. My brother advised me to save many hours of overanalyzing and simply head to the zoo to observe the gorillas.

One of our evening's highlights is usually the "kiss and tell" segment. This is where we really get into the dirt. One steamy night we warmed up with an exploration of the question "Where's the weirdest place you've ever had sex?" One girl answered, "In the back of a parked UPS truck." Another said, "In the middle of the floor of an art gallery after hours." Someone else added, "In the broom closet of a magazine office." (Okay, I admit that was me.)

When the conversation moved to "Who's the most famous person you've ever slept with?" everyone's ears perked up. One girl reported that she'd slept with Robert De Niro, who made "puppy eyes" in bed, then mentioned his incurable case of Jungle Fever. Others described sex with Mickey Rourke ("hot and sweaty") and Perry Farrell of the band Jane's Addiction—"Years ago, we got into heavy foreplay. Suddenly, he stopped and went into a half-hour tirade about sex and the manipulation of society." Another girl told of two nights she spent with Matt Dillon—"He was romantic; he sang Duke Ellington songs to me; he was wearing boxer shorts with 8-balls on them. But he was also a sex maniac! I tied him to the bed, then I rode him. He loved it! He wanted it!" The final tale involved New York artist Jeff Koons—"He was lousy in bed, terrible. He rolled on and rolled off, and he wasn't concerned with me at all." Everyone speculated whether or not his marriage to the Italian porn star has taught him something.

Artists didn't fare well that night. Someone slept with David Salle—"cold, detached, and strange. But sort of interesting." Another recounted her night with the late painter Jean-Michel Basquiat—"He wanted to spank me, so I let him. I thought it would be fun and kinky, and it was. Until I discovered he had given me a horrible case of crabs."

More confessions followed. Someone told of sex with singer Chris Isaak, and a second girl admitted that she, too, had slept with him. They both noted the impressive size of his penis. Their shared experience made them "Eskimo sisters," united by the fact that they had both slept with the same guy. Girl parties further female bonding and give us the chance to compare notes ("Steven got you pregnant, too!").

Every get-together varies according to its participants, but one of our regular features is "show and tell." At the last meeting, our hostess presented a whip made of sewn buffalo testicles. Everyone touched it and screamed. Then someone mentioned the Kegel exercise, a vaginal-tightening technique—"Inhale, count to ten, tighten as you go up the elevator, hold for ten, exhale, and relax." The group did Kegel, giggling and feeling instantly tighter. It was a beautiful thing.

One Saturday afternoon we decided to hold a Gertrude Stein "salon" at my friend's house. In lieu of discussing literature, we decided to upgrade our conversational level to deeper, more thought-provoking subjects. Within five minutes, however, the conversation descended to an all-time low, with sordid accounts of "how we do ourselves," inspired by the fact that inquiring men always seem to ask.

One girl said she had fun with herself while driving a car. "I almost killed myself," she said. "But I liked the idea of coming and going at the same time."

Someone else said, "Once when I was ten I rubbed myself against the carpet. It was a bit rough, but I really liked that deep-pile shag."

There seemed to be a proliferation of women who enjoyed rubbing themselves against inanimate objects. "I like the corner of the couch," announced one girl. "Do you feel compelled to pull over to the side of the road when you drive past a furniture store?" asked another. "No, but the corner of my couch needs to be reupholstered."

A third person volunteered, "I did it against a tree once. I think it was an oak." Another girl remembered her fondness for the family staircase. "I used to slide down the banister and rub myself against the part at the bottom. The teeth marks are still there." Then someone revealed her fondness for her new shower head. "For the past year," she said, "I haven't been singing in the shower, I've been moaning."

Of course, I can't divulge all the things we talk about. It's a secret, you know, just between us girls. What I've revealed only skims the surface. If guys heard everything we discussed they would squirm, stop feeling flattered that we spend so much time delving into their psyches, and run for the hills. They would probably feel embarrassed for their entire species. Men should always remember that women never forget. And that's why we can't shut up.

Poles Apart

A Hard Look at Penises

The gnarly root of manhood, the embodiment of libido, the penis is where life begins. Its mission, discovered during the early phases of puberty, is to spread the seed, conquer the planet, and penetrate the fuzzy void.

To women, the penis is a peculiar organ. We believe that man's best friend is actually his penis. Like a dog, it is always happy to see us, enjoys being petted, and often rubs itself against our legs. When we are not calling it "it" or "he," we are using pet names. An English friend likes to call his "Nigel" or "Cedric"; Marla calls Donald's "The

Donald" or "Trump Tower"; I like to call them "Mr. Friendly," "Bob's Big Boy," "The Violator," or "Thruster."

Up until age four I thought that both my mother and father had penises. Playing with Ken or Barbie made it even more confusing because neither had genitals of any kind, even though Barbie had perky hooters. On the playground, it was the boys' packages that sparked my curiosity. After that, every time my mother took me to the ballet I became hypnotized by the male dancers' crotches. By thirteen, however, I started to understand penises, thanks to local fifteen-year-old boys who were always trying to get me to touch theirs or put them between my legs. That is when I understood that the penis has a mind of its own. As I grew up, I realized it is the mind of a perpetual adolescent.

The difference between male and female physiologies affects the way we view our reproductive organs. Women, with our internal, squishy accommodations, tend to be more self-protective and introspective. On the other hand, men, because of their fleshy protuberances, are constantly reminded of their biological imperative. This might explain why every time I walk by my neighborhood plant store with a man he points to the enormous cacti in the window and says, "There's my size!" Women, conversely, do not walk by a Dunkin' Donuts, eye the hole on a glazed, and make the same comparison.

It's no secret that most men either brag about or exaggerate the size of their maleness. I once overhead a group of guys discussing a friend who was a "Two toweler"—it was so gigantic he could hold up two wet bath towels when erect. According to *Harper's* Index, American men, when polled, claim that the average length of their erect penis is ten inches. The average length of an erect penis according to American women, however, is four inches. Rarely will you hear a bunch of women bragging about clitoris size. ("Wow, Betty—you wouldn't believe how big mine gets! It's almost an inch!")

Women don't make a big deal of what's downstairs, since it's one thing men aren't too judgmental about. We're too busy worrying about the size and shape of our other body parts. But when it comes to genital appearances, men are clearly more vain. Maybe that's why they've built every monument in the world to its likeness. The mighty phallus is represented by erected symbols of power—impressive skyscrapers like the Empire State Building and the World Trade Center and sleek, oblong structures like the Washington Monument. Female genitalia, on the other hand, is associated with holes, ditches, and receptacles. (The only thing I every remember creating that remotely resembled my genitals was a vaginal-shaped ashtray I made in sixth grade.) Men wake up every morning and look at their tools standing at attention. Meanwhile, females rarely get a good look at their genitalia, because to do so, we need a mirror and a searchlight.

Men with enormous endowments think that women worship them. But we cannot idolize an organ, especially if it is attached to someone we can't stand. And, contrary to

Freud's theory, we do not envy the penis. The reasons are obvious. First, we would not know how to sit comfortably with one; second, we do not want something veiny falling out of our shorts; and third, a penis looks terrible in a tight dress.

Whether or not the penis can be considered attractive is a question of relativity. If a man is handsome and sexy, the penis can be very erotic in its surging urgency. We love watching it grow bigger and bigger, like those magic animals that expand when you put them in water. However, if we are sitting on a crowded subway and some creep is standing in front of us shoving his sausage in our face, the penis becomes the ugliest human appendage we have ever seen in our lives. This is not to say that what's between our legs looks any better. I'm the first to admit that what the gynecologist sees all day looks like a slab of hairy roast beef.

Once we have decided to sleep with someone, our thoughts about the penis change. Suddenly, size matters. At this point, we will check out the merchandise, a feat usually accomplished at the movies by accidentally-on-purpose dropping our hand into his lap. Admittedly, a big burrito is more exciting than a little one, but if someone is on the small side we won't necessarily lose interest, unless, of course, we discover a micro-organ. Size is an individual matter; like certain men who crave large breasts, there are women who like giant pipe organs—the bigger and wider, the better. Many women say a six- to eight-incher is most desirable. More than ten inches requires a shoehorn, and a foot-longer needs a crowbar. Ultimately, though, it's not the meat, but the motion. Friends have told me they've had such unsatisfying sex with guys of all sizes that rubbing against a doorknob did a better job.

As far as taste is concerned, the penis is an acquired one, like cognac or fine wine. In culinary terms, it is akin to a salty hot dog with a musky bouquet and a janitorial aftertaste. This is the reason women often carry after-dinner breath mints in their purses.

To discuss the question of circumcision, I surveyed "the girls" one afternoon. Unlike gay men, women don't seem to care whether a penis has a drape or not. The typical response went something like, "Penises look best hard. But a soft, circumcised one looks better than a soft, uncircumcised one, which sort of looks like something out of a medical textbook." Hardly startling news, but that's what girl talk will tell you. The very mention of the word *smegma*, however, brought squeals of "Hold the mayo!" After exchanging stories about poor penile hygiene, the vote swayed in favor of circumcision.

There were two things about penises that our group could not comprehend: men's predilection for grabbing their crotches and for flashing. Neither puts us in the mood. When a man walks down the street grabbing his crotch, grunting something like "This Bud's for you!" we can only think that we are seeing the missing link doing a Neanderthal mating call. Flashing, or as they say in California, "doing the fruit salad," is also curious because one almost has to ask why, out of all the sexual deviations, somebody would choose this. I've been flashed so often, I've resorted to heckling my flashers. ("Buddy, I've seen more meat on a Slim Jim!") It wouldn't be as torturous if they were attractive, but the pervs who hit on me always sport the Larry Bud Melman look. To make matters worse, they'll do it anywhere. Once, while I was sitting on a train, a man on the platform knocked on the window. I looked up and, as the train pulled out of the station, he pulled open his coat. One of those Kodak moments.

The point is, women spend more time analyzing the male mind than we do the penis—we cannot separate the man from his member. We consider the entire person in our arousal. Often you will hear a bunch of guys say, "Let's go out and get some pussy!" Never in a million years will you hear a group of women say, "Let's go out and get some dick 'n' balls!" And unlike men, who seem to get excited by looking at close-up shots of beavers-only, most women say that a man with a bulge in his Calvins is sexier than one who's nude. If women really thought penises were as important as men think they are, we would be reading magazines with names like *Penises Today* or *The Scrotal Review*.

Bachelor Pads

Your Place or Mine?

Men's apartments—they make chills run down a woman's spine, possibly followed by a headache. Women feel about as comfortable in the male abode as even the most modern man would feel sitting amid flowery curtains, frilly furnishings, and lots of pink. The bachelor pad is the anthropomorphized Bermuda Triangle of the single guy's psyche, a masculine environment where women are encouraged to stay for only one reason.

These not-so-domestic dens of iniquity have existed since Neanderthal times, but the bachelor pad as we know it—not so much a place to live as a place to score—surfaced in the 1950s, and its notorious reputation helped put swinging into the 60s. Some things never change, and these days bachelor pads fall into two distinct categories: the superslick pad and the superslob pad. Neither is any place a woman would call home.

Sometimes men and women have opposing views of the world, and their takes on the single dwelling is a case in point. Men see their bachelor pads as a sort of mini-Playboy Mansion. Women see them as Date-Rape Central. The goal of this type of dwelling is to put us in the mood, to get us turned on like crazed nymphos. Hence, the decor combines all the ambience of a furniture showroom with the comfort of a car's backseat. Women do not find this romantic. We hate to be reminded of horny sixteen-year-old boys with hard-ons trying to pull us down onto a car's vinyl seating. This does not make a girl feel special.

The walls are sparsely decorated, hung with abstract art, a Kostabi painting, or a framed lithograph of a 1967 Corvette. The living room is illuminated by sensuous lighting apparatuses—phallic halogen lamps or track lighting with permanently dialed-down dimmers. The home entertainment/seduction center features more than ten remote controls and resembles a control panel at NASA.

The de rigueur wet bar is an ideal podium for him; from there our stud studiously mixes Absolut martinis, boyishly flexing his muscles as he tells stories of recent promotions at "the firm," all directed toward loosening up our inhibitions for some heavy action.

Male fantasies usually have almost nothing to do with what women really want, so by this time the routine is so impersonal and cliché that most women escape to the bathroom. There we find that, like the hairs on his head, everything is neat and in place. A quick peek behind the spotlessly Windexed sliding mirrors of the medicine chest reveals overpriced male grooming products, a Water Pik, Braun shaver, imported condoms, Preparation H, and an early pregnancy tester.

Upon our return he continues his smooth moves by asking if we "want to take a look" at the bedroom with the king-sized bed. On a nearby shelf are a VCR and tapes with titles like *Sperm Busters* and *Lesbian Lolitas*. There is so much planning gone into the room that it's set up like an assembly line where we are "next."

In high contrast to the slick pad is the low-tech slob stable, castle of the casual guy. Walking into a home like this is like tiptoeing through a minefield; the two most frequently heard warnings are "Don't sit there!" and "Watch your step!" Instead of being offered expensive wine or Pellegrino, the only thing to drink is bong water. Typical wall decor consists of graffiti scrawled after a night of recreational drug and alcohol use, swimsuit calendars from two years ago, and some girl's underwear hanging on a nail.

Lighting consists of a bare bulb and year-round Christmas lights. "Mood" lighting is accomplished by artfully covering the bulb with a piece of cardboard. Unlike the superprofessional bachelor with the meticulously indexed Filofax, the slob has phone numbers written in smeared lipstick on matchbooks and napkins. Instead of a designer dog such as a chow chow or a whippet, the only pets in this apartment are in baited traps.

Furniture in the slob pad includes anything that can be dragged in from the street. The philosophy here is major recycling: free is good. Milk crates now contain CD's, a wire spool transforms into a chair, and a stack of newspapers becomes a night table. Accessories include used pizza boxes, a collection of empty beer cans, and randomly placed wads of crunchy Kleenex. Hygiene is not considered a big priority.

While we're trying to figure out how anyone could actually live in such a dump, these guys usually attempt to entice us into dancing the bossa nova as a prelude to easing us onto a lumpy mattress with dirty sheets.

The bathroom, a cootie zone, is a frightening sight— using the toilet safely requires a two-foot hover above the bowl. But it is the kitchen that truly defines slob bachelor living. The refrigerator is a large petri dish where new and exotic forms of life are frequently discovered. The only edibles are condiments stolen from fast-food restaurants. Typical bachelor cuisine is grilled cheese sandwiches prepared with aluminum foil and a rarely used iron.

If women are lucky, some things will change. By the year 2000, women hope that bachelor pads will move into a new era. We would like bachelors to be more romantic, to think of us just a little when decorating. A bouquet of flowers might be nice, and a tampon dispenser in the bathroom would add a sensitive touch.

Whip It Good

Under My Thumb

Pussywhipped: (Poos´e hwipped) *adj.* (1) submissive state of a male who is sexually addicted to one female: the end result of "the best sex he's ever had." (2) a highly sensitive condition whereby a man temporarily surrenders power to a woman; the consequence of being hypnotized by hot poontang.

Only a man would come up with such a retarded, sexist word to describe a relationship that so many people enjoy. Most likely it was coined by a bunch of horny guys drinking beer and watching football while making fun of their friend, who was busy taking out his girlfriend's garbage.

Since the beginning of time, males have dominated females, and this most unnatural he-man inclination still persists. Except when a man is in the whipped state. This is one of the few times when men aren't bossing us around, controlling everything, and creating situations like the S&L disaster or Wall Street crashes.

We like being in the advantageous position for once; it's a nice change, especially when we need our toilets cleaned. We appreciate this eager attitude and enjoy a man who puts out a little effort to please us.

Pussywhipping has existed since Eve forced Adam to bite into the apple, and many men owe their achievements to the PW state, including Napoleon, who was inspired by Josephine.

During the sexually repressed 50s, horny housewives had little political or financial clout, so they had two options. They could either put out for the new mink or withhold sex as a means of persuasion.

By the late 60s, sexual liberation created one big orgy. But it wasn't until the mid-70s, when the sensitive man first made his appearance, that women began exploring their relationship to power. The laws of chivalry and male-dominated society came under scrutiny, and it soon became clear that they were nothing more than some lame excuse for men to have all the fun.

The laws of pussywhipping are based on one simple paradox: Not many men want to yield control to a woman, yet even fewer can resist being seduced by one with erection-inducing capabilities. To some men, a little domination can seem pretty great. He relishes relinquishing control and volunteers for tasks he would never ordinarily do, like putting up shelves. Suddenly, he's a handyman. His girlfriend finds it endearing; his friends think it's pathetic. He's an intoxicated sexaholic, one step away from Pussywhipped Anonymous. Think of James Mason in *Lolita*. Think of George Bush. On second thought, don't.

Becoming pussywhipped is a gradual process. Behavior changes; so does conversation. A pre-PW man would brag to his pals about former conquests and rate women solely on their endowments. Post-PW, things are different. When *she* enters the room it's as if a goddess had just walked in. Suddenly, he is Mr. Polite, and traditional male group behavior like swearing, burping, and farting comes to a halt.

Stage One of PW could be described as the "hot pants" phase. He regresses to an animal-like state and realizes that he can't get enough of that funky stuff. Like Pavlov's dog, he needs intermittent reinforcement and will do almost anything to get what he wants. All we have to say is "Heel, boy," let him suck our breasts, then make him sweep the floor.

Stage Two might be termed "going ape." He calls three times a day, shows up at our door bearing flowers and a raging boner, babbling like Gomer Pyle. He buys a beeper to be at our beck and call. Around now, we begin to implement more difficult tasks, such as having him move heavy objects or sand the floor.

The final stage of PW is "totally pussywhipped," or

TPW. This stage is the most pitiful to other men. As testosterone levels begin to plummet, the TPW man starts doing laundry willingly and is occasionally seen sporting an "I Hate Housework" apron. At this point, even we start to think it's getting out of control, especially when he volunteers to do our hair.

Some studs will never be PW. They want sex with as many women as possible before they turn eighty and are forced to depend on a penile pump. To them, having sex is like having a good workout at the gym; it's part of their daily routine. This is why having men under our spell is a refreshing change. Men who cannot be whipped are not usually as enthusiastic about such things as cunnilingus. The PW man, on the other hand, cheerfully acknowledges a woman's pleasure. Finally, we get to push someone's head down.

The PW candidate is not, however, a wimp. He's just as likely to have gigantic muscles, tattoos, and a Harley as he is to have a concave chest and aquarium glasses. What separates him from the Cro-Mag who can't be PW is that he actually enjoys women's company. He's got spine, but he's not the type who can't wait to leave after the big O. Of course, this also has its disadvantages for women. Sometimes he becomes glued to our couch and we have to send him grocery shopping just to have a little space.

To the man who thinks it's emasculating to become pussywhipped, relax. You'll dig it even though you would never admit it to your buddies, who are home alone with their hands. The pussywhipped man is the man of the 90s.

We appreciate his affection. It encourages us to rush out and buy sexy lingerie and learn those gyrational techniques from the video *How to Strip for Your Man*. We think it's fun to see you panting with manly expectation.

Generation Sex

To Survey with Love

It was a dirty job, but someone had to do it. Someone had to analyze the stacks and stacks of sex surveys sent to male *Details* readers between the ages of eighteen and thirty. I went straight to the sexology office (my bed) and examined the statistical data.

It's possible to know people for years and never know anything about their intimate carnal habits. But give them a form to fill out and they'll tell you everything. After reading the results of this survey, I felt like I had just met 1,254 complete strangers on a Greyhound bus who told me things they wouldn't tell anyone. I now know more than I ever wanted to know about the sex lives of twentysome-thing males—straight, gay, and everything in between. Apparently, the study was more stimulating than anyone expected—in the words of one eager respondent, "I got a hard-on just filling the frigging thing out."

The first question to catch my eye was "How old were you when you first masturbated?" Most guys (75 percent) said they were between ten and fourteen, but 10 percent said age five, 2 percent said age four, another 2 said age three, and 1 percent said age two. At this rate, we'll soon be seeing prenatal masturbation. (Imagine a doctor looking at the sonogram and announcing "It's a boy!" after seeing the fetus chiseling away.)

By the way, hardly anyone skipped over this question, leaving no doubt about the favorite pastime of the twenty-something generation. (One of the surveys was stuck together.)

Although the majority of men described themselves as exclusively heterosexual, there was a sizable portion of gay men among the questionnaire respondents, as well as some who described themselves as bisexual (or "bicuri-ous"). Some bisexuals kept marking different boxes under the sexual-orientation question. After circling all three, one frustrated soul finally scribbled, "Just plain sexual." Only three respondents circled "asexual." Those three also described themselves as very religious, believed that if it weren't for AIDS they'd be less afraid of intimacy, and considered abstinence the only safe sex. They also wished their penises were bigger.

A big surprise was the 17 percent who called themselves "exclusively heterosexual," but admitted to having had a sexual experience with a member of the same sex. Since these guys didn't categorize themselves as gay or bisexual, I phoned a few to see what they had to say. The first man I spoke to, a twenty-four-year-old, said that he and his best friend "both had sex with the same girl simultaneously." He found the wording of the question tricky and explained that in his three-way he "didn't touch the other guy." The second respondent said that when he was eighteen, he and a gay friend once started making out when they were lying on a bed. He kissed the guy to "see what it would be like," but the friend wanted them to get naked. As his friend stripped, the guy realized he really had no interest in men and ran out of the apartment. (Good thing he bolted before getting naked.) A third guy said he once "crossed the line," but then decided he preferred women. A fourth said he answered "yes, once" because his aunt's sicko husband fondled him when he was nine. (That's the last time Uncle Harry got invited over for Thanksgiving dinner.)

My favorite question was one that asked respondents to identify activities they have engaged in such as threesomes, getting tied up, or using sex toys. About a third said they'd tried all three. One statistic encouraging to women who worry about being dumped for someone younger is that 39 percent of the guys said they've had sex with someone ten years older. Even more interesting were the 47 percent who "used food for sexual purposes." (You want fries with that?) Several pencilled in "whipped cream" or "chocolate sauce"; another said he liked "coffee enemas." (Fill it to the rim!) I also called one twenty-six-year-old who said he "liked to use bananas on his girlfriend." I declined to ask where he put the bananas because two minutes into our conversation he started breathing a little too heavily. Only after I hung up did I notice that he answered the question "When you masturbate, do you use any of the following?" by circling "telephone lines."

Men over twenty-two were asked if they noticed any difference between their sex life now and when they were in college. Many said they have more desire now but partners are harder to find; an unfortunate combination.

Sixty-three percent of the men described the frequency they're having sex as "less often than I'd like." The next question asked why. While 49 percent cited "no partner," as the main reason, one divorced male scrawled in the margin, "Wife was a bitch."

Regarding the question asking what drugs were used to "increase sexual pleasure," one lush checked off all that applied—including alcohol, pot, cocaine, Quaaludes, amyl nitrate (poppers), and Ecstasy. Then, filling in "other," he added "mushrooms, LSD, Valium, and laughing gas." The same guy also thought he was having sex less often than desired because of "the immaturity of college women." (I'm sure most women would love to have sex with a coked-out, tripping, Betty Ford candidate who is laughing like a hyena). He also said he had a difficult time maintaining an erection and couldn't tell when his partner was having an orgasm. Duh.

I was relieved to see that 73 percent of men know where a woman's clitoris is. One man scrawled rather defensively, "I've been told I know *exactly* where it is." Gay men, however, were not too enthusiastic about this question: One added, "Don't care."

A big surprise was the response to "Which is more important to you than having a great sex life?" A whopping 44 percent answered "finding someone to love" over "doing well at school" (4 percent) or "pursuing a career" (12 percent). The answers to "Which best describes your feeling toward marriage?" were equally surprising. I thought most men would answer "It's too much of a commitment" (only 8.6 percent did), "it's the death of romance" (2 percent), or "it's a social pressure" (19 percent). But 12 percent said "it's the best way to start a family" and 44 percent said "it's the ultimate expression of love." Still, I found myself expecting to see pencilled-in answers like "makes it harder to have sex with other girls who know my girlfriend."

A few expressed complete dissatisfaction with their sex lives, citing their girlfriends' lack of desire as the problem. One twenty-five-year-old said he often fakes orgasms because of "sexually unresponsive women." Another disappointed twenty-nine-year-old, who described himself as "ex-religious," said that he impregnated his girlfriend, is now living with her and the baby, and complains, "My girlfriend is 'born again' and not too interested in sex. I'm considering another affair." (How about meeting some Mormon chicks?)

I also noticed a number of eighteen- to twenty-one-year-olds who seemed inexperienced or reported they were virgins, leaving half of the survey unfilled. This prompted me to start visiting college campuses, scouting for boys who are "willing to learn." One virgin who wanted to have sex but wasn't getting any cited "rejection" as his reason. My advice to him is to join a weekly support group for sex addicts.

As singles, our biggest fear is of sexually transmitted diseases, so I was curious to see the answers to "Have you ever had any of the following: chlamydia, syphilis, gonorrhea, crabs, herpes, AIDS, or genital warts?" A mere 0.6 percent said they have AIDS—a small percentage, considering the number of friends I know who have become ill. When I saw that 5 percent have had chlamydia and gonorrhea, 2.5 percent herpes, and 5 percent genital warts, I had a paranoia attack as I was reminded that a small percentage of people are still getting those diseases that nobody talks about anymore. More amazing, however, was the 22 percent of the men who said they've had crabs. (I thought I saw something crawl out of one of my surveys.)

This brought me to the "If you are having sex for the first time with a new partner, do you insist on using a condom?" question. Although about two-thirds claimed they did, I had a slight disco freak-out about the one-third who didn't. I was happy to see that most men thought the responsibility of buying penile party hats should be shared, and many kept a stash handy. Most said they kept them in their bedroom, bathroom, or wallet, but a few mentioned that they kept them in their "glove compartment" for some "sex to go." One guy takes safe sex literally and keeps his "in a safe"; another wise guy said he keeps his "on my penis."

Like women who feel insecure about their imperfect body parts, men are worried about their penis size. When asked "How do you feel about the size of your penis?" 6 percent wished it was "much larger," while 36 percent wished it was "somewhat larger." About half said they were satisfied with their tubesteaks. (I kept their phone numbers.) About 11 percent said they wished their penis was "somewhat smaller," and another 1 percent wished they were "much smaller." (Liars.) I didn't believe a penis could be overly endowed until one guy commented, "Hurts females if petite."

Some of the questions seemed to annoy people, like the one that asked whether or not it is "up to a man to make sure a woman is aroused and brought to orgasm." (Most thought it was, which is a relief—now I won't have to do all the work myself.) Some added, "It's mutual." Gay men complained that the question excluded them. A few wrote in "Dumb question."

When asked "Which of the following are your erogenous zones?" dozens added in "ears" and wondered why they weren't included in the first place. Other G spots included belly button, stomach, scalp, behind the knees, and "body hair." Another said "the area between the scrotum and anus," also known as "the tain't." (It ain't your dick; it ain't your butthole.)

All the many wankers out there were inspired by the questions about masturbation. When asked "Do you ever have sex fantasies about famous people?" most straight men voted overwhelmingly for Cindy Crawford. Madonna came in second, followed by Sharon Stone, Demi Moore, Winona Ryder, Drew Barrymore, Michelle Pfeiffer, and En Vogue. One guy said Marsha Brady. Kate Pierson got one vote as did "Hillary Clinton with Chelsea." One person said Whoopi Goldberg. One plebe considered "girls in porno magazines" to be famous.

Gay men went for Jean-Claude Van Damme, Marky Mark, and Dolph Lundgren. Runners up were Brad Pitt, Mel Gibson, Jeff Stryker, Chris Isaak, and Jason Priestley. Al Gore got ten write-in votes. Bisexuals liked River Phoenix, Keanu Reeves, and Prince. One bisexual wrote in "Pee Wee Herman and Sinead O'Connor."

A few surveys stood out, like the one from the guy in prison who claims he's made several girls pregnant, said his balls were his erogenous zone, and thinks his penis is the right size. He confessed he had to "have sex on the sneak. I only had it about fifteen times since being incarcerated." Little does he know he's getting more than most guys on the outside. Another says he uses poppers, often talks dirty during sex, has had every STD, had over twenty partners in the last year, had sex over twenty times in the last few months, was molested throughout childhood, strongly agrees that men enjoy sex more than women, doesn't know where a woman's clitoris is, thinks penis size is very important, has a leather fetish, and enjoys sado-masochism. He also thinks marriage is the death of romance and is too much of a commitment.

After the multiple-choice questions, respondents were asked "In what ways is your generation different sexually than your parents' generation?" Many felt that they are more comfortable talking about sex and have more information about it. They also said that parents have a harder time accepting homosexuality. When asked "What do you regret or resent about sexuality in the 90s?" the general consensus was that people felt they missed out on the sexual revolution. They felt cheated and angry that their parents used to get laid more than they do. Whereas the worst fear of our parents' generation was pregnancy, our generation's biggest worry is AIDS. One master of the obvious wrote, "You could be dead and not even know it."

The question that inspired the most write-in responses was "Do you have a fetish or sexual quirk?" Several responded that sex in public places with the possibility of getting caught was extremely arousing. Another guy detailed his affection for boots: "During my college days I spent a lot of time in restrooms, waiting for a beautiful pair of boots to appear in the stall next to me. After college I started collecting boots again. Two years later I joined a boot fraternity. This has thousands of members and by corresponding with and meeting a few of them I felt normal. I currently have over sixty pairs of boots, a small collection compared to some, but it's growing."

Another guy said his quirks are "small blondes with size-five baby feet—the most erotic sight in the world." A third is turned on by "men in business suits, especially gray suits, with their asses visible. Their vented jackets flap, flop, and ride up with a gust of wind or when they walk up stairs or bend over. I especially get excited thinking of them sitting on a transparent chair and me with a camera underneath." A fourth mentioned women's underwear and "the wonderful smell they hold." Finally, one guy confessed, "It makes me horny to imagine pretty barefoot girls taking a massive shit."

Women have this idea that men only want one thing, but after ruminating on this survey, I was encouraged by the large number who also want someone to love. On the other hand, since nearly half admitted to cheating on their girlfriends at least once, I realized that men are still, in the end, led by the head between their legs.

Which is not to say that all men are dogs. I think they're more like paranoid puppies. They're trying to be monogamous in their twenties, the age at which swingles in the 60s, 70s, and early 80s had sex with as many people as they could until their penises turned purple. (Just ask Wilt Chamberlain.)

Although most guys these days think monogamy is a good idea and say they could even live without sex for a while, they also seem frustrated by a restraint caused by fear of death. What seems clear is that the basic carnal urges have not changed. I got the feeling that, deep down, men would really love to be doing the wild thing way more than they are—and the kinkier, the better.

In the meantime, they are cultivating a rich fantasy life. And they are having loads of sex—with Cindy Crawford, Dolph Lundgren, and their hairy palms.

Silvia Otte

Extremely Single

The Goodbye Girl

Dumping the Boyfriend

You never forget your first love. I never did. Specifically, I never forgot him telling me he never wanted to see me again. My teeth still hurt thinking about how it felt when somebody who I thought was in love with me admitted that he wasn't. It was worse than getting fired (something I had lots of experience with) and closer to being hit by an eighteen-wheeler. Since then, I vowed I would never do this to anyone who loved me. But life shifts gears in ironic ways and a few years later it was my turn.

Dumping the garbage. Dumping a load. Taking a

dump. The word itself has a heartless ring to it. Doing the dumping can be just as painful as getting dumped, as you are the villain pulling the trigger, knowing you are inflicting the pain. How do you explain to someone who really loves you that "I know it's not your fault, but you're starting to get on my nerves."

Most women would give anything for what I had: a big handsome hunk who was affectionate, sensitive, and madly in love with me. The sad part is that being loved is sometimes not enough to counter the increasing incompatibility, the daily fights, and the deep-down feeling that this person is really not right for you. After a couple of years, I woke up one day and realized we had become Elizabeth Taylor and Richard Burton. I knew it was over when I could count the bumps on our heads from our pot-and-pan-throwing episodes.

After I called it quits, he was shocked and felt betrayed. To add to my guilt, the day after we split, I asked a friend to call and see if he was okay. When she reported that he sat up all night looking out a window and crying, my heart sank. I hated breaking his heart. On the other hand, maybe I was flattering myself. Maybe, at this moment, he's at a party, leading a conga line with his new girlfriend who is a supermodel Ph.D. billionairess.

The most noble way to cut someone loose is, of course, in person. This has its drawbacks, however, including the possibility that the dumpee might think you are kidding and return five minutes later with a quart of milk. Breaking up on the phone is a reasonable alternative, sparing you the sight of someone on his knees, sobbing, and begging you to reconsider. The "Dear John" letter is another option, especially if you are a total coward. A letter is also recommended as a supplement to the first two techniques to soften the blow of rejection and momentarily relieve some suffering. The breakup letter should be gentle, soothing, and always take the high road. It's a kind move to say something about how wonderful he was, how you'll miss being with him, and how lucky you feel to have known him. Leave out any mention of the fact that his excessive flatulence gave you headaches.

It is important not to further shatter a person's self-esteem, considering it is probably in pieces already. It's never a good idea to state the qualities you didn't like because taste is arbitrary and the dumpee's next lover might like what you didn't. Nor is it a good time to insult appearance or intelligence. Even if a man thought his ex was inadequate in bed, he should not say, "You know, I've never slept with such a dead fish." Nor should a woman say to a man, "I've seen more sensitivity in a two-speed vibrator."

There is no doubt that the sexes cope differently with getting dumped. A woman's first move is to get together with her girlfriends. She pours out the story, elicits sympathy, and listens to them tell her what a loser he was for dumping her, reminding her that he was conceited about his looks and that his penis was too small anyway. Even if she dumped him, she still needs her friends to reassure her about her decision. Women need time to heal; men, on the other hand, prefer to forget. They dash off to the local strip bar to seek comfort in the cleavage of writhing women with names like Candy Cantaloupes.

Breakups also bring out the voyeuristic side of humanity, the part that likes to watch "A Current Affair." As soon as you tell people about your separation, they behave like rubberneckers at a car accident. They want the dirt. To the nosiest, I merely say, "It's too painful to talk about," denying them the pleasure of lies they were dying to hear, such as, "He had a heavy foot fetish and he was a bed wetter."

Shortly after a breakup, paranoia always sets in. I wondered what embarrassing secrets my ex would be telling about me. I prayed that what goes around doesn't come around, knowing that when my first love dumped me, I gleefully told everyone he was into sucking his own penis.

After a breakup, you start seeing couples everywhere. For the first few days you walk around in a lobotomized *Night of the Living Dead* daze. You experience loss of reality. You consider drinking heavily. To cheer yourself up, you go out and buy a package of condoms, only to realize you won't be needing them. You begin stockpiling Campbell's Soup for One. If you are a woman you rent *An Unmarried Woman*. If you are a man you rent *The Lonely Guy*. Then comes fear: you are convinced you will never have a relationship or, worse, sex with anyone attractive again. Men worry about having blue balls for life, while women fear that all the men they meet will either be in love with themselves or each other. Finally, you contemplate lowering your standards.

Eventually, the two of you will have to meet one last time to exchange whatever you left at each other's home. This invariably leads to sex with the ex, a one-for-the road good idea in the event you won't be getting any for a while. If you are the dumpee, make sure you have a huge orgasm and try to deprive the other person of theirs. If you are the dumper, make this last hump so enjoyable that your ex will forget how much he hates your guts. And the least you can do is not fantasize about someone else.

Single White Female

Looking for Love in the Personals

My long-term relationship was over, my heart was recovering, and my womanhood was tingling. The swingles scene awaited me and it was time to take the plunge, so I decided to join the rest of the horny and desperate losers between the sheets of the personal ads. I chose the *Village Voice* as opposed to the yuppified *New York* magazine or *The New York Review of Books,* which until recently featured men who described themselves as "Woody Allen types."

As I browsed through the columns I realized that reading the personals was a lot like masturbation: it's something you do alone, nobody knows you're doing it, and you feel stupid afterward. Nevertheless, I placed a few calls. One guy said he met all his girlfriends this way. Another told me he thought having a dog was good for picking up girls but reported "You can get laid like crazy doing this!"

There are eight million stories in the naked city and those pages were full of them. I was looking for dates in the "Women Seeking Men" section yet couldn't help but peruse the "Anything Goes" column, which contained ads like "extremely ticklish SHF wanted," "Looking for Bi M or F in need of attitude adjustment," or "pre-ops wanted for erotic encounters."

In the "Multiples" column, people were looking for "couples to watch or be watched" or "submissive sisters/twins a plus."

I noticed a lot of Jungle Fever action, with people describing themselves as "vanilla" or "chocolate" or "caramel," as well as a number of ads that said "Mistress available," "Female college student looking for 'financially secure' Sugar Daddy." One guy in a wheelchair wanted any "eatable" females. The personals were also loaded with "MMs" (married males) looking for "discreet, safe encounters." This section was so huge it should have had its own heading—"Married but Dating." The first ad that caught my eye said, "hot model-turned-therapist, SWM, 30, 6 foot, creative, seeks sweet, deep beauty for romance and consequences." I figured he couldn't be too ugly if he was a model or too stupid if he was a therapist. I called the 900 number, plugged in the extension listed in the ad, and listened to the taped message. He sounded sweet and warm and worth leaving my fake name, "Ann," and a provocative description of myself. He called back, we talked for an hour, and he told me about his work and how he was discovered by a modeling agent on the street. We set up a coffee date. When I saw him I was shocked. I don't mind red hair, but his was cut like Ronald McDonald's. Add to this a set of horsey, discolored teeth, a bad 70s nose job, and bad pants.

As we ate, he tried to be romantic. He cut up his pancakes and attempted to feed me, lifting a forkful to my lips. I held my mouth closed. I wanted to puke. At the same time, I wanted to ask, "So, who did you model for, Barnum and Bailey?" After forty-five minutes of listening to him describe his female patients' sexual advances, trying to impress me with photos of his apartment, and showing me his "recent" press clipping from 1985 and his warped record album from 1981 ("Merry, Merry, Poison Berry"), he was driving me nuts. Then he asked me what I thought so far. I thought he needed a therapist and I needed some Prozac.

My second date was with "a long-haired, green-eyed poet looking for someone sexy butt shapely, any race." He wasn't too bad-looking, but his face dropped when he saw me. "I usually date only black women," he told me, and thought the "butt shapely" part made that obvious.

After this experience, I decided I would have better luck if I placed my own ad. This was free, but retrieving the voice-mail messages cost $1.69 a minute. Establishing the right tone was tricky because every word you use can be misinterpreted: the tone had to be sexy but not sleazy, intriguing yet not appealing to Jeffrey Dahmer types.

Deciding to flatter myself, I wrote an ad that read: "SWF, 29, cool but warm dark-haired exotic beauty with brains (a babe), seeks 30ish SWM handsome and humorous, smart and sweet *Details*-type guy for fun and fire." Then I recorded a provocative voice message under my phony name and said I was entertaining, frequently pumped iron, and got my fashion tips from 60s Italian movies and the old "Star Trek" series.

Almost eighty eligible bachelors—including doctors, lawyers, policemen, firemen, chefs, actors, musicians, "professionals," and a bunch of guys named Shahid or Muhammed—responded. One said, "I'm in the home-improvement industry and details are a big part of my everyday life." Another said he liked "strip poker in a limo." Some people left descriptions of their looks, like "I have a cleft chin and am built about eleven inches up front." One guy described himself as a "four-wheel-drive kind of guy," thinking I might like to join him for a bumpy ride in his Jeep. Immediately eliminated were guys who said they had glasses and mustache combinations, those under five foot seven, "Jeff Goldblum types," and anyone who said he "dressed like Arsenio Hall."

Some people seemed to be reciting their descriptions, like the guy from Brooklyn who sounded like John Travolta in *Saturday Night Fever*, who robotically read that he enjoys "the spontaneity of the city to the adventures of the outdoors."

I called back about twenty people, then weeded them

down to about fourteen dates. My first meeting was with someone who claimed he had "model looks and a genius IQ." We had a nice phone conversation, but when I met him he was actually forty-one instead of thirty-one, had just graduated from film school, lived in a one-room walk-up, did odd jobs, was repaying a student loan, and sported a late-70s swinger look with open shirt and chest hair. He had no personal charisma, but he did have a girlfriend of three years whom he sees on weekends but with whom he "has no physical relationship." Even after I rejected him on the spot, he kept calling me on Sunday nights after his sexless weekends. Eventually, I suggested that he start his own personal column category: "SWL—Straight White Loser."

Hoping to find someone more honest, I made a date with "Bob," who said he was a twenty-nine-year-old doctor. He said he was tall, blond, and handsome, but when I saw him he turned out to have about as much sex appeal as Dick Cavett. He also turned out to be a veterinarian. To start the conversation, I mentioned something about how people get attached to their animals. He responded by saying that owners, when they have to put their pets to sleep, often need therapy. I giggled and he got mad. In fact, he got mad at everything I said. The madder he got the sillier I became. When I finally asked, "Are you turned on by women in dog collars?" he was out the door.

After a few more dates, I realized that most people were either totally deluded about their looks or were liars. I realized that the ads needed to be decoded to their subtexts.

If they described themselves as "attractive," they were

unattractive; "extremely good looking" meant average, "cerebral mensch" meant nerd, "teddy bear type" meant fat; and any comparison to a famous person meant they were the uglier version. One guy told me on the phone that he looked like a young Elliot Gould, but in person was more like Marvin Hamlisch. Someone else who claimed to be a "sexy musician" later told me he was actually an electrical engineer. When I met him, he admitted to reading meters for Con Ed and playing guitar as a hobby.

Looking for someone more dynamic, I called "Tony," whose message said he was a "major New York celebrity, a generous self-made millionaire who loves to buy women presents." I'm not materialistic, but I called him back thinking maybe I'd get a free gift. We arranged a date and he picked me up in a white limo. He looked like a flashier version of Robert De Niro in *Raging Bull*. Over dinner, he ordered a "carajaf" of wine as he explained how he made his money in real estate. The whole time I was thinking about how money can't buy taste. Five minutes later he was telling me how well endowed he was and how other women have told him he "has hurt them with the big one." Tony was not my speed, but I was afraid to leave too quickly, fearing he would send John Gotti and his boys after me. Instead, I told him I had to go home because I was having a heavy flow, and besides, I was still recovering from a bad case of crabs.

After two weeks, fourteen dates, and $335.88 in telephone bills, I still didn't have my dream man. But being the hopeless, pathetic optimist I am, I decided to give it one more try. On my messages that night I heard a deep silky voice with a Southern accent as thick as molasses. It said, "I'm six foot one and I'm going to sound arrogant and say that I look damn good. And don't call me back unless you are drop-dead gorgeous." This sounded challenging, but also too good to be true. When I asked what famous person he looked like, he said, "a cross between Patrick Swayze and Chris Isaak."

We flirted on the phone, telling each other what great kissers we were. And just in case he really was good-looking, I slipped in that I had larger than average breasts. "I have larger than average hands," he replied. I made a date. When I saw him I was pleasantly surprised. More than pleasantly surprised. His description was accurate—he was really handsome. My underpants snapped, crackled, and popped. We had drinks for two hours. At first, he seemed like quite a character. He proceeded to open my beer with his teeth and told me about his exploits while blue marlin fishing, then followed them with a good puke story. Drinks turned into dinner, during which he told me, without my asking, that his father was in the oil business and worth $200 million and that he was personally worth $8 million. "I'm a rich redneck" was the first thing he said that turned me off. Then he told me that he had changed his name from Alan to Ashley. Eight Wild Turkeys later, the veneer had worn thin and his true personality emerged. He talked endlessly about himself, bragged about how beautiful all his ex-girlfriends were, pointed out that he could get any girl he wanted, and said he had slept with over four hundred women. Then he became completely obnoxious, slobbering on my neck, boasting about how he liked to buy drinks for strangers in bars, and how he once blew $8,000 in a night. After he made disparaging remarks about gays and blacks, I accused him of being homophobic and racist. I added sexist to the list when he said, "If women didn't have that thing between their legs, they'd be nothin'." Then he attempted to slip me the tongue, followed by trying to get his thing between my thing. I had to fight him off in the middle of the restaurant.

As I was getting ready to leave, he looked me in the eye and tried to make me promise that I would never write anything about him because he was "planning to run for political office." I suggested he try the Supreme Court.

Have I Got a Guy for You

Meeting My Match(maker)

It was Saturday night and I was becoming hypnotized by the Weather Channel. I called a girlfriend to complain about turning into a dateless hag. We agreed that getting laid wasn't the problem; finding someone who didn't irritate us the morning after was. "We could join a video service like they did in *Singles*," she suggested. "Or we could turn lesbo." I decided to go with the video service suggestion.

I let my fingers do the walking and looked under "Dating." Amid the ads I found a number of listings. One called itself a "personal introduction service"; another promised "video exchanges with selective members." I called several services only to discover that many of the numbers had been disconnected. A few more calls revealed that the New York attorney general's office had closed some services down for fraud and overcharging. I reconsidered the escort option.

Finally, I found one that answered. The ad read "Field's Exclusive Dating Service. Meet new people! Love, Friendship, Happiness." I asked the man why he hadn't been closed down. "Because you pay me, you get results. Come right over, I'll give you five men today!"

Stepping into Field's office was like stepping into a time warp. In the foyer hung a tinted photo from the 30s of "Uncle Sid," sporting slicked-back hair and a pencil mustache. The walls were covered with seventy years' worth of marriage photos, wedding invitations, and kitschy bride-and-groom paintings that would look great next to a black velvet Elvis. A sign dating from the 30s said, "This is not a lonely hearts club, this is a matrimonial agency exclusively for friendship and marriage."

Mr. Field appeared, a sixtyish man with hornrim glasses who looked like Larry King. "Come in! Sit down!" he said, checking me out. With a Yiddish accent that sounded like Jackie Mason he said, "An attractive girl like you shouldn't be alone. You should get married, settle down, have a couple of kids." Suddenly, I was in *Fiddler on the Roof*. Behind him was a sign: "The best-looking and most well-educated people have the hardest time finding lasting romance," reassuring applicants they weren't pitiful losers.

"Look!" he says, pulling out a stack of cards from his files. "I've got attorneys, I've got businessmen! This one's worth millions!"

"I'd prefer creativity over tons of money," I said.

"You don't want money?" he asked incredulously.

"Well, first I want somebody smart," I said.

"The men who come here are smart—they're not married!" he delivers with Borscht Belt timing. Then he asked where my parents lived.

"Maryland," I said, "outside Washington."

"I've got men in Maryland, I have men all over. Men I have, there is no shortage of men! Here's a guy from Maryland," he says, pointing to a graduation photo of a cadet from the Annapolis Naval Academy standing at attention. He looked so stiff I wondered if his bayonet was stuck up his tuckus. "Why go out looking when he's right here!"

"Um, do you have any more photos or videos?" I asked.

"Ah," he grunted, "when you meet them you see their picture. Nobody looks like they do in photographs anyway."

That's when I noticed a bulletin board filled with photographs of eligible bachelors and bachelorettes. From the looks of this wall, the sign should have read, "This service is for people who haven't had a date in years." I also realized that the only thing "exclusive" about Field's was that everyone pays $500 and fills out a card.

"Give me $500 and I'll give you five names right now!" he pushed.

"I'll have to think about it," I said.

"What's to think about? A nice girl like you should get married, settle down, have a couple of kids," he repeated. "I accept cash."

"I don't have cash," I said.

"I'll wait for you to get the money out of the cash machine."

At that moment I realized I would be nuts giving $500 to get dates from a man who pushes like a used car salesman and looks like a Catskills comedian.

"How much do you have?" he asked. "I'll take a $100 deposit, a $50 deposit—"

"All I have is $5," I said, showing him.

He grabbed the bill out of my hand. "You can pay me the rest tomorrow," he said as he repeated for the millionth time, "a nice girl like you should get married . . ."

After Fields, I searched for another matchmaker with more potential. I looked under "Matchmakers" in the Yellow Pages and called the one listing. It turned out to be a dog-breeding service.

In the back of *New York* magazine, I noticed an ad for a woman who described herself as "New York's Premiere Matchmaker." Under a photo of a young model-looking blonde, it read, "Are you someone special who isn't meeting that special someone? Don't be discouraged. If you are successful, sincere, emotionally mature, and ready for a permanent relationship, please contact me."

When I called, a woman named Denise answered. She promised to find me the man of my dreams, who I'd get the old-fashioned way—by paying for him.

I made an appointment and went to her apartment, in a swanky building where I was greeted by a white-gloved doorman. Upstairs, the door was answered by a woman with bleached hair in a pink jogging outfit, Denise's mother. She announced that she was her daughter's "image consultant." She was also going to sit in on our meeting because she was "in training" to be a matchmaker. As I looked at the wedding invitations strategically placed on the coffee table, Denise told me that ten couples she introduced have been married and eleven couples were dating. She was quick to point out that she was legitimate and has never been accused of anything illegal. She told me that each applicant is "prescreened," which means that if I were accepted I would be required to take an AIDS test and have my educational record investigated. She would also check my criminal record. I flashed back to my wild teenage years as a juvenile delinquent and wondered how my record of charges ("minor in possession of alcohol, indecent exposure") would look now.

After some preliminary questions, she asked me what age I was looking for.

"Twenties or thirties," I said.

"How about someone around forty-five?"

"Too old," I said.

"How about a *young* forty-five?" piped in the mother.

"What was your childhood like?" Denise asked.

"Fun, happy," I said. She looked disappointed.

"You know 99 percent of people come from dysfunctional families," she told me. "Would you consider going out with a person who has lots of problems but has been working them out for the last twenty years?"

She probably had a real mess who she thought was perfect for me. The more we talked the more she tried to convince me that I should be "flexible." Then I asked what her fee was. When she told me I almost fell off her nouveau plush couch.

"Ten thousand dollars," she said.

"That's a little high for me," I said.

"Maybe your parents could help you out," she suggested. "Think of it as an *investment*. I'll be your friend, your 'love coach.' I personally go out to parties or art openings, pick out men, and arrange an introduction."

For "an additional fee," she told me she would do "special searches" out of town. At that point, I realized that a matchmaker is something between a personal shopper and a pimp.

The third matchmaker I contacted preferred to be called an "executive heart hunter." She told me over the phone that her service is for "successful overachievers who want to find a more meaningful relationship. For them, I provide social management," she said in yuppie-speak. Her service, which cost $2,000 for two-and-a-half years, included a subscription to *The Highly Classifieds*, a monthly newsletter listing one hundred hopefuls and their lengthy personal ads. She asked who else I had contacted, and when I said Field's, she said, "He's right out of a Mel Brooks movie." When I mentioned Denise, she dished,

"She used to work for a matchmaker named Helena who was indicted for fraud. I wouldn't consider either of them my peers. With my service, I let people choose each other, then I become their 'guidance counselor,'" she added. "It's the processed and filtered way to meet someone," she said.

I was used to my coffee filtered, but not my men. I came home and read the ads. One said, "The only way to picture me is to imagine Alan Alda snorkeling." A second read, "This 50s-looking 65-year-old looks like Fred Astaire." Another said, "If you have tortoise-shell glasses, I'll book the hall!" The last one said, "Most importantly, my future wife needs an overwhelming desire to start and operate a major international corporation. My company creates computer systems products and I need a wife able to manipulate, coerce, and motivate people within reasonable morality." (Wanted: a computer with tits.)

Continuing my search, I found a service advertised as "The uncommon dating service with world-class introductions." Run by Jessica, a sweet woman in her seventies, the $700 fee seemed like a bargain by comparison. This included a "lifetime membership," which didn't guarantee much, considering her age. A former concert pianist from Chicago, Jessica has been a matchmaker since the 40s, when she first fixed up a buxom brunette with a gangster. Envisioning a young mafioso sucking my breasts, I wrote out a check.

Once I was signed up, the dating tips segment began. "Think of peaches and Scarlett O'Hara," she said. "You don't want to come off too strong, that can be intimidating to a man." (Little did she know—I've been known to light my farts on the second date.)

"And don't judge on looks alone," she warned.

"Guys do it, why can't I?" I asked.

"Because, my dear, you'll be a bachelor girl for a long time."

Then she gave me a brochure that she wrote, which included "The Golden Rules of Dating" with advice from 1942 like "Avoid the mention of chronological age. The issue of age is always a sensitive one." (Translation: "We have lots of old guys who want young broads.")

Then she said, "Anka, you're a lovely girl with a lovely face and darling figure, but your hair is going to take some getting used to." (Translation: "It would be easier setting you up if your hair didn't look so slutty.") Finally, she lectured me on disease protection ("use two condoms") and sent me out to meet my future husband.

I didn't have a clue what Rich looked like because Jessica kept her thumb on his photo while describing him. All I knew was that he was a thirty-eight-year-old investment banker who wanted "someone from a good family who could be a social asset." When he called, he described himself as "very all-American, very good-looking, sort of like Gidget's brother." When we met, I tried not to look disappointed. He was very thin, with thick aviator glasses, not much hair, and even less of a chin. He could have co-starred in *Gidget Goes to Nerdsville*.

He started talking a mile a minute, proving himself to be a

real "Hello, how am I?" kind of guy, never stopping to ask me anything. In the first five mintues, he reeled off his personal resume ("My father's a lawyer, my mother's a professor, I have an M.B.A. from Yale, a house in the Hamptons . . ." blah, blah, blah. Then he tried to impress me by telling me how investment bankers like him, in the "upper echelon," are really geniuses. Bored, I steered the conversation to other topics. Everything I mentioned, he topped. "Mozart is the *only* music I listen to," "The St. James Hotel is *so* much more civilized." When I brought up movies, he got cranky. "I don't see what was so funny about *Wayne's World*. I walked out." At that point, so did I.

Bachelor number two was Dan. At forty-two, he was older than I wanted, but as Jessica told me, he was someone I "shouldn't pass up." Dan was a classical flutist who played in the symphony and wrote advertising jingles on the side. He sounded great on the phone, but when I walked into the café to meet him, my hopes plunged. He was half bald, had a mustache, a barrel chest, and a fat stomach. The worst part was that he turned out to be very likable. We discussed the nature of creativity, insanity, and Camus. He was so charming that for a second I fantasized about having sex with him with a bag over his head. The date ended with him saying, "You look like Winona." Instead of graciously accepting the compliment, I blurted out, "Wynonna Judd?"

My third bachelor was Tom, a thirty-four-year-old doctor who specialized in liver transplants and tissue research. I made the mistake of saying, "Tissue research, how interesting!" and he launched into a monologue about isolating tissue cultures. After fifteen tedious minutes, I changed the subject to avoid slipping into a coma. To liven things up I asked, "When they do sex-change operations from male to female, do they really stuff the meat back up in there?" He was not amused.

Next came Irving, a man who Jessica told me "doesn't date much," but who made $500,000 a year with his employment agency business. Irving was in his mid to late forties with a graying ponytail and an oversized nose. After three minutes he asked, "So, do you think I'm cute?" Ten mintues later he asked, "So, are we falling in love yet?" Then he started doing magic tricks, embarrassing me as we sat in an outdoor café.

At that moment, my friend Christian spotted me sitting there and plopped down with us. Irving pulled out more tricks, including the "pick a card, any card" number that forces participation, followed by the disappearing coin and handkerchief tricks.

My friend Christian was so uncomfortable that he had to get up and leave. As he said goodbye, he looked at me with one of those expressions that said, "What are you doing with such a clown?"

When he finally put away the magic handkerchief, the conversation turned to the 70s and drugs. He told me how he was heavily into Quaaludes back then. Unfortunately, he didn't have any with him; I could have used some just to get through the date. When I said I had to leave, he insisted on walking with me. Then he dragged me into a toy store, bought some plastic balls, and juggled them in my face all the way home.

The next day, Jessica called to tell me, "Be patient, this was only the first batch." If these guys were the best of the lot, I cringed at the thought of the worst.

Phone
Mating

Lure of the Rings

I didn't know what I would find on the party phone lines, but that was part of the excitement. Who calls these things? I wondered. Maybe it would be like "Love Connection" on the phone. Who knows? I thought. Maybe Mr. Right was out there, calling the line for a goof. On the other hand, with my luck, I'd probably fall in love with someone's great personality, and he'd turn out to be a dwarf.

First I called 1-900-999-EASY at ninety-five cents per minute. The TV ad for this line begins with the camera zooming in on the biceps of a hunky guy talking on the phone in a steam room. Then the camera cuts to the cleavage of a girl coming out of a swimming pool. I eavesdropped for a while, but soon realized it would be more stimulating if I participated in the conversation.

"Hey, baby," said a macho-sounding guy from the Bronx who sounded like Sylvester Stallone. "Why don't you give me your phone number?"

"Describe yourself first," I said.

"I'm very attractive," he said, "and I only date very attractive women."

"What do you do?" I asked

"I'm a porcelain salesman," he said.

"You mean, like toilets?" I asked.

"Uh, yeah," he said.

"Groovy job," I said, unable to resist.

Another girl came on the line and he convinced her he was a catch as she wrote down his number. Another male voice came on the line and asked me to describe myself. After I gave a provocative description of myself, male voices suddenly appeared out of the woodwork.

"So, Anka," said some guy named Bob from Yonkers, "do you like Broadway theater?"

"No," I said.

"Do you like to ski?"

"No."

"Do you like to spend afternoons with small children?"

"No."

After I said no to three more questions, he said, "So, Anka, why don't you take down my number?"

Another guy with an anxious voice got on the line and said he was twenty-three and from Queens. He asked me where I lived.

"Manhattan," I said, "SoHo."

"Ooh, wow," he said. "Does that mean you're an artist chick?" (Translation: loose and kinky.) "That turns me on!"

"No, I'm a writer."

"Oh, that means you're probably not that great looking."

"I write pornography," I snapped. "Does that make me sound any better looking?"

After calling two more lines—the Party Line and 1-900-CHAT—I realized that I had to set up my own rating system based on answers to my interview questions. "I live in Brooklyn, Queens, Staten Island, or the Bronx"—minus three points; "I live in New Jersey"— minus five points; "I sell plastic tablecloths"—minus eight points; "I'm married"—minus fifteen points; "How you look?" "Where you live?" or "I ain't got no job" (incomplete sentences or bad grammar)—minus twenty points.

I decided to try out my rating system on a Saturday night at three in the morning. I called 550-GABB after seeing a commercial for it. This line lives up to its advertising image and demonstrates that as price goes down so does quality. The ad features a Crazy Eddie spin-off in a white polyester suit, dark sunglasses, and a plastic straw hat with a telephone on top of it. "This is Crazy Gabby!" he screams over noisemaker sounds in the background. "You'd have to be crazy to pay ninety-five cents a minute when you can pay twenty cents for the first minute, ten cents after that!" As a blond bimbo in a bikini blows a horn and makes cooing sounds, he yells, "Let the party begin!"

As expected, I found this line to have the highest percentage of Neanderthals per minute. Callers were drunk and sounded even more undesirable than the callers on the other lines, even though it was 3 A.M.—apparently horny happy hour.

"Hi, this is Mike," said one voice. "Any females out there?"

"I want pussy," said another male voice.

"Any nymphos out there?" asked a third.

"Right here," I said, real sexy.

"Who said that?" they all asked.

A girl named Allison got on the line and everyone thought she said it.

"Allison, how big are your breasts?" someone asked.

"They're, um, nice," she said, not knowing what to say.

"I'm all tied up," said a guy in the background, "and I'm playing with my wiener."

Suddenly I was part of a phone orgy.

"Do you like to give head?" asked another male voice.

"Only if it's big enough," I threw in.

I hung up before I lowered myself any further.

I called 550-GABB a second time in the middle of the afternoon. Most of the people were calling from work, running up the phone bills of their unsuspecting employers while pretending to be working. After I described myself as "really hot-looking" to some new prospect named Steve, some other guy asked, "If you're really so hot-looking, why are you calling up this line for dates?" Before I had a chance to respond, he hung up. Then a few minutes later, I recognized his voice and heard him arrange to meet a girl at Forty-second Street and Eighth

Avenue. "I'll be wearing jeans, a T-shirt, and Reeboks" he told her, a description that will have her wandering around one of the worst neighborhoods in New York City all night.

A guy named Tom who described himself as a "Wall Street consultant" called from the offices of Merrill Lynch.

"What kind of name is Anka?" he asked.

"It's Yugoslavian," I told him, not wanting to go into the differences between Serbians and Croatians.

"You don't sound Yugoslavian," he said.

"Maybe that's because I'm American. What are you wearing?" I asked.

"A pin-striped suit, white shirt, red tie, and wing-tip shoes," he announced proudly.

"I like to wear black," I said.

"If you came into Merrill Lynch for a job interview wearing all black, they would never hire you," he said anal-retentively.

"I don't want to work at Merrill Lynch," I said. "I'm too bohemian."

"Bohemian," he said. "Is that in Yugoslavia?"

This guy was denser than the toilet salesman.

"I'm hanging up now," said an irate female voice in the background.

"Oh, but why," said another voice, both eavesdropping on my conversation with Tom.

"I'm hanging up because *someone* is dominating the phone conversation," she said.

"Maybe *someone* else doesn't have anything interesting to say," I said.

She hung up. Suddenly I felt like the big phone dominatrix.

After I'd had my fill of the Gabb Line I called the Fresh Line. In the ad for this line two fly girls are sitting in a hot tub talking on the phone. The camera moves to a brother talking on the phone in a steam room. The next shot shows all three of them in the hot tub.

As I came on the line I heard, "Hello? Who's this?"

"This is Melika. Who's this?" a woman answered.

"This is Darnell. Melika, do you have a big butt?" She laughed. I laughed. Darnell laughed.

"Do you have light skin or dark, Meilika?" asked Darnell.

"I'm dark chocolate," she said.

"Ooh," he said, "the darker the berry, the sweeter the cherry."

Three other guys got on the line, including one who sounded white. The black guys tried to push the white guy off the line by calling him a homo. When he hung up, the remaining two guys tried to get each other off the line by calling each other homos.

Next, for some teen spirit, I called the Teen Line. The commercial for this shows teens talking and giggling on the phone in their bedrooms, stuffed animals in the background. One of the girls says, "You like Bruce? Everybody likes Bruce."

When I called, most of the conversation went something like this:

"So, whaddya doing?"

"Nothing."

"I'm bored."

"My parents aren't home."

As I listened to these nonconversations, my mind wandered to a newspaper story I read about some kid on Long Island who called the Teen Line and invited hundreds of people to his parents' house while they were out of town. They caused $25,000 worth of damage.

The second time I called 550-TEEN, I overheard two sixteen-year-old Puerto Rican girls making plans to meet in a parking lot to beat each other up. Then I head a forty-seven-year-old guy named Herman searching for jailbait.

"Why don't you give me your number?" he said to Susie, who is seventeen and a cheerleader.

"You're too old for me," she said meekly.

"Get off the line, Grampa!" yelled a male voice.

Finally, I found a line that was somewhat dignified. On the Intro Phone an operator asks who each new caller is, introduces that person to the others on the line, and asks preliminary questions. It was sort of a civilized phone dinner party. When I called I met a female radiologist and two males (a lawyer and an emergency room doctor). They were so civilized that I found myself trying to stay awake.

Just as I was about to hang up, however, a nineteen-year-old goofy kid called up who said he played drums in a band, went to NYU, worked part-time at MTV, and wore nipple rings. I acted interested in him, so he told me how the night before his cat accidentally walked into the refrigerator, and in the morning, when he opened it, the cat walked out, shivering with icicles.

"You sound cute," I said, "but a little young for me."

"I'm an excellent student," he said.

I took his number.

After calling all these lines I thought I'd had enough. But like any new addiction, it has to be done just one more time. So I called 1-900-999-LUCK.

"Hello, who's this?" I asked.

"This is Jeff."

"Hi, Jeff. This is Anka."

Again, I hear five guys on the line, vying for one female.

"What kind of guy are you looking for?" asked Jeff.

"I want someone handsome, cool, and intelligent," I said.

In unison, they all hung up.

The Young Girl and the Sea

Cruising the Love Boat

A few weeks ago my sixty-two-year-old neighbor told me she met a new boyfriend on a Caribbean cruise. She assured me that she was now getting more sex than I was. Hearing this, I decided to shop for the perfect cruise—fun, sun, rum drinks with little umbrellas, and half-naked people doing the Forbidden Dance. Then my Singleworld cruise brochure arrived in the mail. "Nonstop fun," it promised, "sparkling entertainment and fabulous meals. Maybe that's why over 300,000 single people have fallen in love with us." I envisioned balmy nights of romance and magical ports of call. Then I looked at the attractive funsters on the white Caribbean beaches sitting on each other's laps, dancing to steel drums, and wrote out a check for $1,890. Two weeks later I was off for a seven-day cruise of the high seas, on my way to "mega ship luxury" and "the time of my life."

As the shuttle bus drove through the Puerto Rican countryside from the San Juan airport to the ship, I looked around to check out my fellow vacationers. "Hey!" said a Joey Buttafuoco look-alike to his buddy, "this place looks like Brooklyn!" "Nothin's pink in Brooklyn!" said his friend as their group howled. I prayed these people would not be boarding my love boat.

As the passengers boarded the massive 46,000-ton boat, the ship's photographer snapped their photo. Everyone seemed to think this was exciting, but it made me instantly paranoid. Especially when one mother and her teenage daughter pointed at me, giggled, and started singing the theme song from "The Addams Family."

Once in my cabin, a card awaited me from Skip, my Singleworld tour director, encouraging me to meet my singles tour group—or as my brochure said, my "very special travel family"—in the Ain't Misbehavin' Lounge at 8:00. My group consisted of eighteen women and two men, many with nine-to-five jobs as dental hygienists, secretaries, and physical therapists. Two small-town girls from North Carolina, Marybeth and Katherine, took an instant disliking to me. My new "family" was dysfunctional.

Wanting to remain anonymous, I wondered what I would tell the group I did for a living. I contemplated posing as a gynecologist but decided against it, afraid that women might start making me listen to the details of their yeast infections. Then I thought it might be amusing to tell the group I was a proctologist, but didn't want to put up with being the butt of asshole jokes for a week. After watching a parade of crispy tops and slacks that made me want to announce "Attention, Kmart shoppers," I decided on "fashion writer."

According to Singleworld, Skip would be "our guide, our advisor, our ice-breaker." Skip was a twenty-six-year-old hunky blond surfer from California, with large pectorals and shiny, happy white teeth. Especially impressive were his credentials as a former Studs contestant. The two other bachelors were Gary, a thirty-five-year-old film editor from L.A., and Harry, an awkward thirty-eight-year-old tax accountant from Michigan with bad posture who could only be described as "the Dork." Harry instantly attached himself to me like a barnacle.

I fantasized about an adventure set aboard an elegant ocean liner of the 1930s, a Noël Coward scenario where the men were sophisticated, the women chic. Instead I discovered Middle America aboard a crowded fourteen-floor floating hotel/mall in Vegas. The decks were packed with honeymooners from Indiana and retirees in comfy leisurewear, as well as tour groups of insurance salesmen and Finalube (oil lubricant) conventioneers from Texas.

The first evening's dinner began with a welcome from the ship's crew and the introduction of the captain and his four-year-old boy, both sporting white dress uniforms. "Father and son look like Ricardo Montalban and Herve Villechaize from 'Fantasy Island,'" I said to Skip, who whispered in my ear,

"Do you know what pickup line Herve Villechaize used on women? 'Gee, your hair smells terrific!' "

I figured I wasn't having too bad of a time if the first night's conversation included suggestions of streaking through the dining room, references to dangling hemorrhoids, and speculations about whether hymen reconstruction was available in the ship's beauty salon.

As the ship sailed to Martinique, the major activity of the day was the Single's Mingle, where all the unattached people on the boat of almost 3,000 would congregate. I went mingling with Sandi, a secretary from New Jersey who was seriously looking for a husband. Her face dropped when she saw that the mingle consisted of our group plus ten fugly women and two cute guys who instantly left because they either thought the scene was a sorry sight or were in love with each other. Sandi was having a major bad time. I told her to cheer up and that we could always crash the Honeymooners' Get-together at 7:00 and try to pick up some couples who were into threesomes. ("Swingers' Mingler.") Then, as a last resort, we could go to the Grandparents' Get-together at 8:00 to meet some sexy seniors.

Our first island hop was Martinique. In the morning I went on a guided tour with my group to see an extinct volcano and drive around the island. By this time, the two women from Minnesota were so desperate for a single man that they kept snapping pictures of themselves with the cab driver, exclaiming, "I just love black men!" as if they had never seen one before.

As the tour continued, they even got out of the car and

took a photo of themselves with a cow. I still have not figured out the significance of this. Afterward, Skip told everyone that "the people in Martinique are snotty and unfriendly, they speak only French, and everything is expensive." In true ugly-American style, everyone got scared and went back to the boat by noon. I went into town myself and had a great time buying cheap kitsch items and meeting a cute French guy from Paris who was extra friendly and spoke English. I even got to try out my French from a joke phrasebook I bought: *"D'accord, Pierre, mais garde-toi d'ébouriffer ma coiffure."* Translation: "Okay, Pierre, but be careful not to spoil my hairdo."

That night, my fellow passengers were all complaining about the false promises made by their travel agents, who told them the boat would be filled with "lots of interesting single people." The contrary was true—the boat was a single's nightmare, made worse by an overabundance of kissy-face honeymooner couples.

The two dental hygienists from Minnesota who invested their savings in the trip came to dinner looking like they were on the verge of tears. The film editor was wishing aloud that he had booked a Club Med vacation. The two office managers from Syracuse thought that a single's weekend in the Catskills would have been an improvement.

I wasn't feeling as pessimistic. I was still sweating from my recent flirtation in the Casino Royale, where I made bedroom eyes with a sexy black-haired, blue-eyed croupier. Then there was always Skip. Skip was sexy in that handsome but vacuous soap-opera-actor kind of way that seems fresh for about one night. Apparently the radiologist from Utah thought so too, because the next morning I saw her crawling out of his cabin with a huge sucker bite on her neck.

If it's Wednesday, it must be Barbados. That day we all headed for the Jolly Roger Pirate Ship Cruise, an excursion around the island on a fake 1492 pirate ship. According to Skip, there would be lots of party action with bachelors and bacherlorettes from all the other cruise ships docked in the port. For once, he was right. The Jolly Roger was packed with fun-worshipping kegger hounds determined to party until they puked. As soon as everyone hit deck, a bunch of steroided guys stripped to their swimsuits. Three minutes later, I was cruising the shores of Barbados with 300 sets of pecs and breasts in my face. The Calypso music was cranked up and the boat sailed off. Over the loudspeaker came the news that "The bar is open!" as 300 party animals cheered as if somebody just won something. After two drinks I was instant wreckage. A second announcement was made warning against "friggin' in the riggin'." Next, the captain told everyone to give a big "hi!" and shake hands with the person next to them. Suddenly I was Miss Congeniality and wanted to shake hands with everyone on board. Soon everyone was wearing cardboard pirate hats and dancing to "Hot, Hot, Hot." A conga line formed. I looked to see who was behind me and it was the Dork, grabbing my hips like he was ready to mount me from behind.

Once everyone was lubricated, the boat docked and another announcement was made for those who wanted to "walk the plank." This meant being blindfolded by some guy dressed as a pirate, tied up, and forced to teeter on a wooden board into the water. In my state, jumping into the sea blindfolded with my hands bound behind my back seemed completely logical. After I plunged in and then climbed back on board (I got to keep the blindfold and rope for later), the Dork told me how kinky my jump had looked. "You liked it, huh?" I asked. "Yeah," he said. "I'm into punishment. That's way I joined Singleworld."

A few minutes later I started talking to one of the two cute guys at the Singles' Mingle. He also happened to live four blocks from me in New York. He was a thirty-year-old brain surgeon, a sensitive guy trapped in a macho body, traveling with another doctor and having a terrible singles' cruise. He told me how he accidentally spilled rum on some guy's feet, which were covered by blisters and second-degree burns, then analyzed the mental capacities of the Jolly Roger passengers. His combination of brains, beauty, and bootie made my swimsuit bottoms wetter than they already were.

Two hours and several drinks later, Doctor Bob and I were back on the ship's pool deck, lying in a lounge chair, shamelessly slipping each other tongue. It was getting hotter. As we publicly dry-humped, our hormones started pumping and certain organs began to swell, including our bladders. Since water sports were the theme of the afternoon, we ended up peeing on each other in the pool. He started it.

The Jolly Roger expedition seemed to loosen up my fellow travelers—or at least to lower their expectations. With only three days left to cruise, desperation was setting in and everyone started eyeing the help. One night, we confessed our flirtations. The physical therapist admitted the Barbadian cabin steward with the gold tooth liked her. The film editor described his intrigue with one of the ship's female photographers. One of the dental hygienists kept hugging the dining room steward, whom we dubbed Romeo. I admitted that every night I went into the casino for a cheap thrill and made eyes with the dashing Blackjack dealer who said he was willing to risk his job by sneaking into my cabin after work.

I couldn't help but notice how pathetic we seemed—a group of horny singles on a crowded boat fantasizing about the employees. It was like going to a black-tie party hoping to meet someone interesting and ending up fingering the waiter's hors d'oeuvres.

By this time, the girl from Utah and Skip were acting like Honeymooners. The Dork confided to me in private that he put a glass to the wall and listened to them doing it the night before. He also noted that afterward he had sex with himself and that it was good.

The next morning we stopped at St. Martin/St. Maarten, a half-French/half-Dutch island. Eager to bake my white butt, I asked a cab driver to take me to a nude beach on the French half. We drove through the countryside to a secluded beach, where he dropped me off in front of a sign that said "Orient Beach—a naturist resort. Visit our hotel, beach, and shops." It suddenly hit me that this was not only a nude beach, but a real live nudist colony. I've been to nude beaches before, but I had no idea that nudist colonies still existed. The concept seemed about as anachronistic as a singles' cruise.

For the first five minutes I thought I was having a dream

where everyone was walking around naked. It was like being in a "Star Trek" episode where the crew lands on Planet Nudeon. An elderly couple in their seventies walked by holding hands. They were wearing hats and sunglasses. A couple in their fifties appeared, whose huge behinds needed a "wide load" sign.

The salespeople and customers in the T-shirt shop seemed completely unaware of their exposed hooters and members. As I watched them I realized that nude shopping makes perfect sense: There's no need to take off your clothes, no dressing rooms are required, and there's no need to ask anyone's size.

I bought several T-shirts, one depicting a silhouetted man developing an erection and another one illustrating various breast configurations including "Flap Jacks," "Pointers," "Bee Stings," "Block Busters," and "Double Bubbles." By this time, my gift shop purchases were beginning to have a running theme.

After my shopping spree I went into the restaurant. I recognized a young couple from the boat because the wife had sneered at my bra dress the night before and had said to her husband, "What kind of outfit is that?" Yet here they were, the next day, dining in public stark-naked, thinking nothing of institutionalized nudism. I ordered a papaya drink, which was served to me by a woman with pendulous, papayalike "Has Beens." I prayed she hadn't used one of them to mix my drink. I looked at the menu and hoped I wouldn't spot anything like "Soupe Testicale." Adding to my culinary distress were the chefs in the kitchen, who were cooking in the raw. I hoped that in addition to the law "Employees Must

Wash Hands," they also had a requirement forcing workers to wear nets on their pubic hair.

I sat on the leatherette chairs and started to sweat. I wondered if the restaurant had someone spraying each chair after use, like the guy who sprays the shoes at the bowling alley.

Suddenly losing my appetite, it was time to hit the beach. On the way, I picked up some brochures advertising nude snorkeling and wind-surfing expeditions. I also noticed an ad for "Skinny Dip Travel," an agency specializing in nudist vacations. I wondered if the people at the travel agency were all naked too. I walked down the beach to take in the scenery and eyeball people barbecuing their genitalia. I looked at all the penises, noting length, width, head size, circumcision status, and veins. I also checked for dingleberries and spotted a few cling-ons.

Further down the beach, a beautiful woman was sunning as three tourists with camcorders zoomed in on her shaved clam. Apparently, they were the Beach Beaver Patrol.

A few hours later, I was in pain. I was burned in places where it's said "the sun don't shine." That night at dinner, the film editor was telling everyone about his experience at the nudist colony. He reported excitedly that he met two cute naked girls with perky breasts. They were from Holland and made plans to visit him in Hollywood, where he said he was a big film mogul. The Dork was bummed that he missed out on the nudist colony and instead paid a rip-off artist $60 for a submarine tour that made him extremely claustrophobic and brought him close to a nervous breakdown. But, for some reason, he wanted to know if I had seen "more white or black penises and which ones were bigger."

"I don't know," I told him, "but I saw some big ol' blue balls."

"I've had those all week," he confessed.

The fifth day we stopped at Antigua, where I learned about the sexual habits of the natives. This place should be called "The Friendly Island" because every cab driver was more than willing to reveal the intimate details of his love life. En route to the beach, past the Caribbean Christian Broadcast Station and restaurants advertising "goat soup with souse" and "cow heel stew," he explained to me that the Caribbean man has a "vicious tool" and that Caribbean women "like it from behind." He also said that the island man "explodes like a volcano." I made a mental note to book my next vacation here.

That evening was Formal Night. Doctor Bob and I started off the evening watching other passengers line up to take formal photographs à la Sears Portrait Studio. For a minute, we thought we were at someone else's bad prom. After dinner, we ventured into the Dancin' Lounge for some "dazzling Las Vegas–style entertainment." Jacqui, a cruise staffer (and an former Miss Asheville, North Carolina), was leading the karaoke, warming up the crowd with "Puff the Magic Dragon." The first singer, an André the Giant clone in a tuxedo and Finalube name tag, sang "The Closer I Get to You" with real sensitivity and a touch of Elvis. Then a newlywed couple, he in 80s "Miami Vice" wear and she in a glittery "Star Search" dress, sang a duet of "How Wonderful Life Is

When You're in the World" with tears streaming down their faces. A woman who was very serious about her singing career—most likely performing in order to say she entertained on a cruise ship—belted out an off-key rendition of "Do It to Me One More Time" to shouts of "Yea Doggie!" Mesmerized by the succession of bad acts and stimulated by the hum of the vibrating ship under our seats, Bob was feeling romantic. He suggested we take a cruise for our honeymoon.

Our last day at sea, Bob and I snorkeled and smooched in St. Thomas by day and tried to hide from the rest of the Singleworlders at night. Unfortunately, he didn't try to grope my pants, and we went back to our separate cabins. The next morning, as Bob and I strolled off the boat together holding hands, I waved good-bye to my droopy-faced and still-single Singleworld friends. Marybeth and Katherine muttered under their breath, "So long, Skanka!"

To my disappointment, I never did hear from Doctor Bob. A month later, I saw him on the street walking hand-in-hand with another brunette. Two weeks later, however, I did get a cassette of love songs in the mail along with a heart-shaped card thanking me for "the good times we had together." It was from the Dork.

Road Testing

Prophylactica

Becoming a Condomaniac

Condoms—those unromantic latex devices that sanitize us for our protection—are a boy's best friend. Condoms have become an essential part of the modern man's wardrobe, an extra sock for the third leg.

Despite their hygienically and politically correct ubiquity, condoms are not a modern phenomenon. Back in the Middle Ages, slaughterhouse workers discovered that animal intestines conveniently fit over the penis. (I hate to think how they realized this.) In 1564, Fallopius, discoverer of the Fallopian tubes, advised men to wear linen condoms, which were tied at the base with a red ribbon.

Many ascribe the clinical name for the rubber to the court physician to King Charles II (1160–85), Dr. Condom, who was knighted for his invention of a sheath to prevent the birth of more illegitimate children. Others speculated the word was derived from the Latin *condere:* to cover up, protect, preserve. The most notorious supporter of the condom was Casanova, the legendary eighteenth-century Italian lover, who not only wore them but also blew them up to amuse the ladies. In 1839, Goodyear vulcanized rubber, making it stronger and more elastic, thus paving the way for the modern condom. The invention of synthetic latex one hundred years later ushered in a new era of comfort. During the 40s, in a wartime effort to save rubber, nylon condoms were tested on soldiers, but were found to produce too much static electricity.

Since that time, the embarrassment the men face when buying a prophylactic has not disappeared. Today women and men are buying condoms, sharing both the responsibility and the shopping experience. While some men were raised to believe that a condom in their wallet was a badge of playboyhood, women now slip them into their handbags as a matter of convenience and safety. Our only problem with shopping for condoms at the drugstore is the inevitable sudden appearance of four male salesclerks who emerge from the woodwork, eager to serve us. This makes us even more uncomfortable when we're standing in front of boxes with names like "Climax," "Night Rider," and "Deep Stroker."

As with choosing lovers, one should be selective about condoms. Keeping this in mind, I decided to road test a few brands with a "willing volunteer." First up was the Vibra-Rib condom, which, according to the package, provides "extra raised ribs" that promise "an added dimension of pleasure for her." I have no idea what the guy who invented these was thinking about, but we tried them, and instead of experiencing "pleasurable friction," I felt like I was being pumped while driving over speed bumps.

Mentor brand condoms are advertised in women's magazines and marketed directly at females. Housed in a small package resembling a pudding snack-pak, Mentors featured an "applicator," a thick, ribbed, flesh-colored rubber hood that looked like a cross between a receptacle tip and a baby-bottle nipple. According to the instructions, I was supposed to slip the applicator over the erection and squeeze it to create an airtight seal. The sight of this contraption not only dampened the romance of the moment, but made the penis look like it was wearing a lampshade on its head.

The same reaction occurred with Fiesta condoms, which come in assorted bright colors. These made my research assistant look like he was wearing penile party balloons. Glow-in-the dark condoms, however, were great for home entertainment. When all the lights were off and the neon was thrusting, it had a strobelike, disco effect. Bareback condoms assured him, "You'll hardly know it's there. It's like wearing nothing at all." They were right—it broke. At that point, ecstasy turned into paranoia.

For the sake of our mutual health, we tried the opposite extreme: any condom that said "extra strong" or "sturdy to resist breakage." Though I barely noticed the difference, he complained that these felt like steel-belted radials on his penis.

Kimono condoms from Japan pledged strength and effectiveness, but neglected to mention that anyone even slightly well endowed would be unable to fit one over the head of his manhood. My big man tried one, and it popped off, leading us to believe we had just sighted a UFO. Luckily we found Kimono Plus, for the "larger man," along with Trojan-Enz Large, Maxx, and Magnum, all directed toward men who have a big gun in their pants.

For dessert, we tried mini-flavored condoms. ("It's a condom, it's a mint, it's a condomint! Try Ramses with Retsyn!")

Since condoms are here to stay and we must live with them, think of them as being on your side, your latex buddy. One solution to the problem of timing and application is to install your own "family-planning centers." Try Velcroing condoms to places where sex may occur: the bed, the couch, the kitchen table, the door. Then get accustomed to using condoms by simulating your own field maneuvers. Develop a quick-draw skill, like soldiers who have to take apart and reassemble a rifle in the dark.

The female condom, which consists of a piece of plastic covering a rubber rim, has not yet gained popularity. This may be due to the fact that, for the man, it is like porking a Hefty trash bag. But some diligent researchers, intent on refining and further developing the condom, are hoping to create what they call a "unisex condom." This, according to the National Women's Health Network, "is a latex, diaper-like device to be worn by either male or female." Kinky.

Prophylactica II

Future Sex

On a recent trip to the drugstore, I noticed the condom section had grown bigger and bigger. This meant it was time to update my prophylactic repertoire, so I called my "research boy," who willingly came over for more scientific experimentation.

As we condom shopped, we bought anything that looked new and/or perplexing. One condom looked like it was made of steelwool and had a disclaimer on the front that said "For novelty purposes only." "Let's get one of these," I said, until I noticed that it also said, "May cause severe hair loss."

We brought our purchases home, spread them on the table, and decided what to use first. Starting with the pack of dental dams, my research assistant went to work. After trying out the small squares of pink latex, he reported it was "like licking a plastic tablecloth." Next he slipped on the original French tickler, a pink condom with tiny nubs on its sides. This was obviously designed by a man because the only thing this tickled was my cervix.

Still in the novelty mood, we pulled out the happy condom. I had the choice of the "hand" or the "cacti" version. Not wanting to insert anything resembling a spiny cactus into my reproductive system, I opted for the hand condom. When this was put on, it looked like a miniature plastic glove sitting on top of the penis. Instead of participating in any sort of stimulating foreplay, we spent the next five minutes making obscene hand gestures with it. This was followed by my research boy doing the wave with his organ.

Next we tried the Zulu condoms—"Designed with the black man in mind," according to the box. When unrolled, these looked like they were designed for Long Dong Silver. Apparently, someone decided to make a profit from a cultural stereotype. Staying with the erotic ebony mode, we tried an opaque black condom. When pulled over the erect male member, it looked like a cross between a miniature stealth bomber and a penis in scuba gear.

Now we were ready for something more hardcore. Thinking the female bikini condom might be kinky, I couldn't wait to try one. I especially liked the accompanying literature that said, "The bikini condom puts a woman in charge of her own body. This product is sure to revolutionize how both sexes appreciate protected passion; i.e. safe sex."

Whistling the theme from "How to Stuff a Wild Bikini" as I stepped into my bikini condom, I anticipated this device to be naughty in a Frederick's of Hollywood kind of way. With a slit in front and back, it looked similar to my favorite Frederick's mail-order item—the crotchless panty. I ebulliently sang Helen Reddy's "I am woman, hear me roar" as I made final adjustments to my "women in control" product. This contraption consisted of a latex bikini panty with a tube-shaped internal condom. (Instead of "underalls" I was wearing "inderalls.") Instead of feeling sexy, I felt like I had just stepped into a plastic grocery bag. Because it was slightly lubricated, I also felt like I was wearing a pair of wet Huggie diapers.

"Probe my plastic void!" I exclaimed to my boy. "Beach blanket bingo!" he yelled. Then he cooed "You're my baby," as we continued communicating in baby talk. We quickly progressed to light spanking. (This is called infantilism.) The bikini was turning out to be kinky, but not in the way I expected. The actual use of the latex contraption, however, was somewhat distracting. As it moved, it made a rustling sound like someone playing with a plastic bag in a movie theater. The most disappointing aspect of my "woman on top" device was the fact that by the time it was over, instead of feeling "in control," I felt more like a sanitary landfill.

A few hours after this anticlimax, we were ready for more product research. The brochure explaining the Reality condom made promises similar to the bikini condom. "For the first time, American women can be in control," it said. "Never before in the 400-year history of the condom has this been true." It explained that "a woman can manage it herself." It also predicted that "Reality is never what you thought it was going to be."

The Reality condom consisted of a thin polyurethane sheath with two flexible rings at each end. It looked like a combination between a regular condom, a diaphragm, and a vacuum cleaner bag. This female condom seemed even more industrial than the bikini condom and was filled with gooey, dripping lubrication made from silicone. Putting this thing in felt like I was suiting up for Chernobyl. At first glance, it looked like an amoebic Ziplock freezer bag filled with antifreeze. The best thing about the Reality condom, according to the instructions, is that "Reality can be inserted long before intercourse, up to eight hours." This is useful if you're walking in a bad neighborhood and are worried about getting gang raped, or if you ever plan on getting so drunk that you lose your motor skills but still want to have sex. The instructions also pointed out that the "Polyurethane is more resistant to tears than latex." This was a relief; since there's little chance of a blow-out, I can leave my "fix-a-flat" repair patch kit in the glove compartment.

Inserting the Reality is a task that requires just enough work to interrupt the in-progress sex act. In our case, this resulted in a "Hollywood loaf" (a half hard-on). By the time everything was situated, the genitals appeared to be hermetically sealed. At this point, it looked like a coffee filter crossed with a mini-trampoline. Foreplay with this thing on seemed remote. Inserting the penis into Reality was like guiding it down a waterslide at Action Park. But then again, penetrating Reality is always a trip.

It was like being probed with a slimy synthetic sheath made from the stuff they varnish floors with and filled with the gunk they make fake boobs out of. Besides this, it made noise. According to the instructions, "Noise can be reduced by adding a few drops of lubrication." I said to my boy, "Excuse me honey, while I go to the powder room and oil my bag."

Once the Reality condom was loaded up, the only thing I felt like I managed was someone else's waste products. Pulling it out was like pulling out a water balloon filled with man-splooge. Twisting the outer ring had the same feeling as closing a lawn and garden bag with a twist tie.

Maybe this device should be called the Surreality condom, or the Alternative Reality condom, or maybe the Virtual Reality condom—"You can see it, but you really can't feel it."

Sometimes fantasy is better than reality.

My Camcorder, My Self

Video Head

I am eleven years old and my father is filming me cartwheeling and somersaulting across the living room with his 8mm home movie camera. I am on a roll, until suddenly my braces get stuck in the shag carpeting. Mom runs in to cut me loose as my fall from grace is preserved on vintage celluloid. My recent screening of this footage from childhood inspired me to capture those special moments of adulthood. So I bought a camcorder, put it on a tripod, and within minutes was filming myself dancing naked to "Car Wash" and waving to the camera with my breasts.

At first, I took my camcorder everywhere, an attempt to document life in the 90s for my future children. I took it to a baby christening, a family wedding, and a roof party where I filmed street hookers lifting up their skirts and getting into cars while party guests tried to figure out whether or not they had penises. Next, I started filming such non-events as street evangelists urging uninterested pedestrians to rid themselves of "Coors and whores" and people walking their dogs in designer sweaters, talking to them like human beings.

The camcorder made even the mundane interesting. Suddenly, I was shooting arty close-ups of my orifices. Next I progressed to filming my sphincter blowing smoke rings. I realized I was becoming self-indulgent when I started documenting any large or unusually shaped bowel movements. I knew I was becoming obsessive when I filmed my third monster dump of the week. At this point, it occurred to me that I should get a life. It also made me realize why I was still single.

The camcorder offers immediate gratification, which is perfect for the narcissistic 90s. And nothing brings out narcissism and vanity more than a three-dimensional camera. Most people fantasize about appearing on television, but they don't realize that the small screen is also the rudest mirror. After years of convincing yourself that your nose is just fine, there's nothing like a camcorder to remind you that it's bulbous and filled with blackheads. One male friend reported that after seeing his stomach overhang on the screen, his self-esteem was lowered. He called the experience "humiliating." He was also disappointed when he saw his penis on the screen. He thought it would have looked bigger, considering the camera is supposed to add ten pounds.

The camcorder also brings out any exhibitionist tendencies people may have. When I took it to the Wild Girls Club, it polarized everyone into either camera-shy or camera-hogging. Filming a group of twenty, half the girls ran out of the room while the other half came to life with the slightest encouragement. They wanted to be actresses and I wanted to direct so I told each of the ten girls to fake an orgasm while groaning into the lens. This was followed by a dramatic group climax. It was the feel-good movie of the year.

The idea of camcorder as sex toy intrigued me so much that one night I decided to film myself doing the wild thing. But since I had no partner, I had to love the one I was with. Playing with yourself can be reason enough to feel like a loser, but seeing it amplified afterward is even worse. Not only did I appear incredibly lonely, but my overgrown public hair looked like one of Cher's wigs.

Adding to my sexual frustration, later that night I overheard someone having sex. Suddenly the nosy neighbor, I put my ear to the walls and floor trying to determine where the moans were coming from. It sounded like the neighbor I met recently; the one who was a computer salesman, had a subscription to *GQ*, and liked blondes. Two nights later, while talking to a girlfriend who wanted to go out and look for love connections, I heard the sounds of sex again. Within minutes, I was climbing out onto the fire escape, following the trail of groaning and slurping noises to his open window. Lying on my stomach, I turned on the camcorder and spotted a hairy butt through the lens. Then I saw my neighbor's huge penis being licked by a beautiful blond, who also had a large penis. I zoomed in on his mouth.

As I lay there scrunched under the windowsill catching all the juicy action, I thought to myself, "I am a pervert. A techno Peeping Tom. I need professional help." It didn't stop me from watching, however. I was transfixed, enjoying voyeurism at its best as I watched the other guy shoot his manly deposit into the air, some of it landing on a lamp. An hour later I ran into both of them in the grocery store. They were buying mouthwash and Crisco. I went home and recharged my camcorder battery.

For those without dates, the camcorder's most useful function is as a pick-up device. For guys, it's a prop that gives you that lost-and-vulnerable-tourist look when you're asking for directions from someone you want to have sexual intercourse with.

If I hadn't been carrying my new toy, I wouldn't have found a co-star for the action adventure film I wanted to make. He was sitting on a bench in the park filming anyone goofy who walked by. I fell in love with his extraordinary chin. (It was the only part of his face I could see behind his camcorder.) When our eyes finally met through our viewfinders, I saw my video-dating dreamboat. We talked for two hours and I told him I was documenting my life. He told me he was shooting a home porno movie. We made a date.

That first night, I filmed the tattoos on his arms and the back of his neck. I didn't let him kiss me, but I did tongue his camera lens. On the second date we watched a boxing match at a friend's and I asked him to film my girlfriend and me as we staged a female boxing match followed by a hair-pulling cat fight. This was an attempt to turn him on. The third date we put the camera on the tripod as I progressed from sitting on his lap to no-charge lap dancing. On the fourth date, we went into production. It was so exciting that our feature film became a short.

Compared to the thrill of filming, watching the tape afterward was a major anticlimax. "We look pretty sexy here," said my cam man at first glance. Then he watched himself roll over onto his stomach and yell, "Where's my ass! I have absolutely no buttocks!"

"At least yours doesn't have zits on it!" I cried. "Mine looks like a pizza butt!"

Then he screamed, "My scrotum looks hideous—like two wrinkly tea bags!"

This led me to the conclusion that human genitalia and anything surrounding it are not particularly photogenic. Especially when I noticed that my own crescent of love actually looked more like a sliced baloney sandwich with sprouts.

The next night my co-star volunteered to act in more scenes. I introduced him to my favorite erogenous zone— my fire escape—and made him unzip his pants while I filmed him groping himself. The camcorder created a distance that gave me more freedom to direct him to do something depraved, like watering my flower box. As he held his hose, I looked up at the building next to mine and saw a naked man looking out the rear window through binoculars. This gave new meaning to the term "neighborhood watch."

Our short was turning into a full-length feature, so we decided to give it a title. We considered naming it after some of our most esteemed porn video titles (*The Sperminator, Top Buns, Malcom XXX, Broadcast Nudes*), but decided on *Naughty Neighbors*. For our next scene we took lines from some of our most cherished TV movies, like *The Amy Fisher Story*.

AMY: "Oh, Joey, give me a lube job—you promised."
JOEY: "Amy, you're so young and buff, let's try some Turtle Wax."

Then we added touches of amateur videos, where real-life couples have real sex with real dialogue like, "Let me get on top," "Bend over," and "Hand me that towel."

For our soundtrack we used the Kentucky Fried Chicken "Finger Lickin' Good" jingle and the theme from *Grease*. We also simulated a scene from one amateur video where the camera-shy lover gets self-conscious in front of the lens and loses his erection—an Academy Award–winning performance.

When shooting was finished, it was time to edit our

film. First, I spliced my *Home Alone* scene with clips from this year's Miss America pageant. Next, I cut segments of my neighbors with nature shots of two armadillos having intercourse. Then I slipped choice moments from the Rob Lowe video in with the shriveled erection segment. For the finale I intercut Jimmy Swaggert's "I have sinned" footage with the fire escape masturbation scene. *Naughty Neighbors* is coming to a theater near you.

Camcording II

Voyeurism, the Sequel

Two weeks after my acting and director-ial debut, I filmed a promotional trailer for *Naughty Neighbors*. It was a Saturday night and I was getting ready for a hopefully hot date. In the middle of my push-up bra and lipstick application, I once again heard the melodic sounds of sex. Grabbing the handycam, I jumped out onto the fire escape in search of more eyeball-poppin' action. I had to move fast, because like any sex act, you never know how long it will last.

I peered into one neighbor's window; he was alone and scratching his butt. I snooped into another's; she was watching a "Stop the Insanity" infomercial and picking her nose. As I peeked into a few more windows, the sounds got louder until I discovered the heavy breathers. Focusing, I pushed the "record" button. Then I turned up the microphone to pick up the squishy sounds.

Standing on the fire escape, barefoot in the freezing cold, I watched the fornicating couple. Suddenly, the guy looked up toward the window and for a second, I thought he saw me. At that moment, I envisioned being arrested for Peeping Tomism and being a public nuisance. This prospect added to my sick and cheap voyeuristic thrill. Then I thought that if he pressed charges I would make a deal with him that he could peep on me if I could peep on him. Then we could all go on "Donahue" together: "Peeping Toms who peep on each other."

My neighbor didn't see me because he was too busy pumping away with all the sensuality of a store mannequin. Presumably his partner liked it this way, because she was making appreciative dolphin noises. I watched him pump faster, stop, and then look satisfied. I couldn't tell if she was satisfied or not. If I couldn't tell, he probably couldn't either. It was none of my business whatsoever, but there I was speculating. They never switched positions until he got up to smoke a cigarette. It's one thing risking arrest to see a stimulating sex act that you're not supposed to be watching, but it's another story watching two people having bad sex. But I guess peepers can't be chosers.

Love Drugs

Is It the Motion or the Potion?

Aphrodisiacs. Just saying the word gets me excited. When I think of them I think of Cleopatra in her boudoir mixing up a love potion to turn on Marc Antony. I think of the notorious people throughout history who used them: Don Juan, Casanova, Balzac, Henry VIII, the Marquis de Sade. I look at the strange collection of exotic plants, herbs, and roots I have just bought and wonder what they will do to me. Will they change me from a horny girl to an uncontrollable sex-crazed nympho? Will I become perverted and kinky? I hope so.

By definition, aphrodisiacs are "agents that stimulate

the sexual appetite and function by direct or reflex action on the genital centers in the brain and spinal cord." The word derives from the name of the Greek goddess of love and fertility, Aphrodite, and they are as ancient as the missionary position. They were used by the studly Hercules, who supposedly deflowered fifty virgins in one night; by King Tut, who was buried with them in his tomb; and by Roman royalty, who, at banquets, had them kneaded into bread to help get the postprandial orgy going.

In America, oysters and Spanish fly are the most well-known aphrodisiacs, but their effects are questionable. Raw oysters do contain high amounts of zinc, which increases prostate function, but not necessarily horniness. Spanish fly is a tincture prepared from crushed flying beetles that is taken internally or rubbed on the genitals. It may stimulate some, but it also causes heavy irritation, painful burning, and huge, oozing blisters. Real sexy. Other dubious concoctions include rhinoceros horns, crocodile teeth, and partridge brains.

Personally, I prefer a more herbal approach, so I sent $2.00 for my Of the Jungle catalog, where botanical herbs, spices, roots, and plants from all over the world, including the Amazon and African rain forest, are sold. I heard about it from a granola friend who not only mail-orders his aphrodisiacs from there, but his hallucinogenic cactus seeds as well. This probably explains why the company has no phone number (P.O. Box 1801, Sebastopol, CA 95473). I then recruited an enthusiastic "potency volunteer" for my study with one stipulation: If either of us got turned on, the other had to put out.

When my shipment arrived I was already wet. First I tried guarana, a rain forest shrub still processed by the indigenous people of Brazil. A little too anxious, I misread the directions and used two tablespoons of powder instead of two teaspoons—three times the recommended amount. I started to take off like a rocket and felt compulsively driven to sanitize my bathroom, wash all the windows, and defrost my refrigerator. Sex was the last thing on my mind. Guarana made me sweat like a pig, made my voice quiver, and gave me the shakes. When I started breaking into uncontrollable Katharine Hepburn impressions, I became such a turn-off that my laboratory partner had to rent a porn video to continue the experiment by himself.

Montezuma's Secret, described in the catalog as "an underground sensation," looked more promising. In 1520, Cortes burst into the Aztec court of Mexico and found dirty ol' King Monty busy poking the royal harem, which he kept aroused with his secret brew. It consisted of cocoa seeds (which supposedly contain phenylethylamine, a chemical produced by the brain when people are in love) and fiery hot chilies blended with roots including matico (a stimulating Peruvian herb) and damiana. I boiled up two tablespoons in a pot of water and, after downing what tasted like a cup of red peppery rust, a hot rush flooded my system. After twenty minutes I started to tingle "down there." I thought I was imagining this until I went to do my laundry and suddenly, Me So Horny. I had a compelling urge to ride the Maytag during the spin cycle. Back in my apartment, I realized the first rule of aphrodisiacs: Don't take them alone. Even the knockwurst in the refrigerator started to look good.

My faith restored, I moved on to straight damiana. This herb, which grows on small shrubs in the deserts of Texas and Mexico, is said to be a "reproductive organ rejuvenator" that works by increasing blood flow to the capillaries. One cup and I wasn't sure what my ovaries were up to, but my clitoris was doing the mambo. After my research assistant drank some, his organ sprang into action and he chased me around the room.

After a week of downing these elixirs, I began to notice a few side effects. Damiana doubles as a diuretic, which means it stimulates urination. This did not interfere with my sex life, but I realized that if I drank two martinis, I'd become an instant Depends user. I also noticed an increase in energy and endurance, both in and out of the waterbed, and an influx of erotic dreams. One night, I dreamed I was in my Maidenform bra at Anka's harem, filled with cute guys who were performing oral sex while showering me with flowers, compliments, and kisses—any woman's fantasy, especially the compliments.

The last thing I tried from Of the Jungle was gold root, a toothpick-size root used by Mexican herbalists for toothaches and teeth cleaning. The catalog suggests chewing a matchstick-size piece to "create an intense tingling sensation on the lips and mouth that can be used erotically; as the sensation can be shared from mouth to other skin areas." I chewed a piece and my mouth began tingling and buzzing; similar to Novocain but less numbing, more organic, and more hallucinogenic. My mouth felt like it was stoned. Then I transferred some to my volunteer's penis. He said it made his penis feel stoned. Then he chewed a piece and licked my you-know-what. It felt hot like someone put pepper on my pudenda. The only trouble with this substance was that during the few minutes the sensations lasted, it made us both salivate like rabid dogs.

With my hunger for sex increasing along with my appetite for experimentation, I went to my local herb store for some more cheap thrills. Charlie, my consultant, told me to give my man the Male Libido Compound, a "tonic" of Korean ginseng (a stimulant for longevity and strength), sarsaparilla root (a testosterone enhancer), and saw palmetto (a berry that invigorates the sex glands) for three weeks. "It will make his balls grow," he promised. He also told me that tonics combine ten or fifteen herbs and work slowly over several months to strengthen the adrenal glands, "nourish and tone" the sexual organs, and stimulate circulation.

I brought home the tonic and told my man about its testicular effects. He looked scared, but drank it anyway, relieved that it had a pleasant herbal taste. After a week, he noticed a rise in night boners and a slight heaviness in the testicles right after drinking. "Remember calling up bowling alleys and asking if they have fourteen-pound balls?" he asked me. "Now I have them."

The second tonic we tried was the "unisex" Lycium

Sexual Elixir with lycium berries and jujube dates (a chewy fruit). After two months of drinking this sweet tonic, we found it more moving than exciting, particularly in our large colons.

My last stop was the Chinese herb store, which carries many aphrodisiacs like crushed deer antlers, rattlesnake, and Shum Yung Oi Ow Bing pills, containing extracts of the private parts of sea otters, donkeys, and dogs. The Chinese have used these strange concoctions for centuries, ever since they discovered their goats nibbling on some mysterious weeds and then mounting each other uncontrollably. I figured they must know something that I don't.

I liked the sound of Fo-ti-tieng, a favorite of Li Ch'ung-yun, who supposedly lived 256 years and was still fertile when he keeled. He also had twenty-four wives and an erectile potential NASA would envy. Unfortunately, this root, like codpieces and jockstraps, is for men only. It reportedly boosts sexual vitality, "promotes male character," and increases sperm count. My man tried it but didn't notice any special effects until he ejaculated and felt like he had a fire hose between his legs. We both noticed more semen on my face than usual.

Jim Radakovich/Courtesy of the Museum of Natural History

Sexology

Pillow Talk

What You Say Is What You Get

It's a language unto itself, those romantic utterances made by couples sharing intimate moments of nooky bliss, ranging from a simple "You're the only one" to "Honey! Let's get out of the leather swing and cat mask!" Unfortunately, when it comes to mastering this particular tongue, most of the male species are in need of a speech therapist.

Some men will say almost anything to get a woman into bed. This is the time when they are extremely talkative, most charming, and more articulate than they've been all day. Suddenly, what's in their pants has an effect on what's in their brain, and vice versa. But by the time a woman's clothes are half off, a curious thing happens: men become momentarily speechless.

Flattery, the verbal equivalent of foreplay, is important. Unfortunately, women and men have totally different ideas of what that is. Men seem to like it when women compliment them on the size or shape of their privates. Women, on the other hand, do not need to be told, "You have a beautiful pussy." Women pay so much attention to their appearance that being complimented on their genitalia is low on the priority list. It is the equivalent of being told we have an attractive anus.

"You're a *Playboy* fantasy come true" is another common male ploy. A woman's translation of this one is: "You are a total sex object. You remind me of the photos I used to look at when I started masturbating at age twelve."

Oral sex presents other semantic difficulties. To man, sperm is "nature's love juice." To women, this substance is as appetizing as a glassful of runny boogers. Men don't understand why we don't like it. So pillow talk such as this ensues:

HIM: Doesn't it smell like the ocean?
HER: I was thinking more of a toxic spill.

Conversation during intercourse emphasizes the business at hand and frequently includes such classic expressions as "That feels good," "Harder," "Higher," "A little to the left," and, finally, "Bingo!" This is a time when most words seem unnecessary. Even ordinarily intelligent men regress to animal states when fornicating and may emit deep barnyard noises. It is also a time when women, more often than men, are notoriously loud. Women do appreciate it that men are tolerant of this.

But a man's true character is revealed after sex, when women find out whether their guys really like them, or if they are total jerks. Depending on the situation, women feel either vulnerable, emotional, or romantic after sex. They want to share togetherness. Some men, however, seem more concerned about their fluid loss and may say, "I'm thirsty. Could you get me a glass of water, babe? I'm about a quart low." Other men revert to more childlike behavior. After sex, this type of guy likes to sit closely in front of the TV. He may exclaim, "These Flintstones are really good! I love Barney!" while laughing like a six-year-old and eating Cocoa Pebbles from the box. Moments like these are especially horrifying to women who realize they have just copulated with a moron.

The love-'em-and-leave-'em type is just as bad. These men can't wait to get into bed and can't wait to make an exit. They have no interest in engaging in any conversation other than "Where did my socks go?" With these guys, any smoothness they demonstrated before sex goes out the window once the act is over. Nevertheless, these simple men have a way of lowering a woman's self-esteem in five seconds with such sensitive observations as "Gee, I didn't realize you had such a big butt!"

To sophisticated women, the jock mentality is the

worst. To jocks, sex is merely a workout, a physical experience rather than a bonding one. "Let's party and get naked" is a typical opening seduction line. During sex they narrate as if they were at a sports event and were their own cheering section. They might yell, "Go, go!" or "Yeah! Yeah! I'm coming into the home stretch! I'm almost there!" By this time the woman is so turned off that the only thing she can think of is sending this guy to the bench. These men usually forget one thing: the female orgasm. Their climax is usually followed by a slap on the ass and a line like "You're a team player!" before they roll over and go to sleep.

Women don't want men to speak to us in bed like we are one of their sports fans. Women want gentlemen who aren't afraid to make pillow talk sweet and sexy. We want men who shower us with sincere compliments, not insulting, dumb-guy statements. We want sensitive lovers who know how to express themselves—a cross between Romeo and Phil Donahue. And we don't want to be told to sleep on the wet spot.

The Joy of Tape

How-to Sex

N ow that I'm dating but not yet playing hide-the-salami, I wanted to further my adult education and that of my future love machine with self-help sex-ed tapes. According to *Better Sex Videos,* "Know-how is the best aphrodisiac. The more you know the better it gets." I imagined how good it might get and called the 1-800 number. Excited to improve my technique, I then dashed to the How-to Video Source, a store specializing in instructional videos of all types. Past the New Age and hypnosis tapes, I found the sequestered sex tapes an inch from the floor in the "Parenting and Sexuality" section.

I grabbed any video that said "contains nudity" or "encourages viewer experimentation." As I piled up $300 worth of tapes on the counter, I couldn't help but wonder what the cashier thought of me as she fixated on the one titled *Sexual Problems.* At this moment, I realized that instructional sex videos could replace condoms, Preparation H, and adult diapers as the newest embarrassing purchase—when I'm buying condoms, at least I look like I know what I'm doing.

Feeling pitiful for watching tapes marked "couples only" by myself, but anxious to become a better lover, I began with *The Great Sex Series.* Volume III was hosted by Dr. Frank Sommers, a "psychosexual" therapist with a Dracula-like accent and a creepy voice, who has assisted "many couples seeking help for all kinds of sexual difficulties." Andy and Andrea, a "real couple," began with a warm-up dance, then undressed each other, revealing his white Sears briefs and her control-top panty hose. Dr. Sommers narrated as the two Frenched, fondled, and took a bubble bath to lounge music. This kind of hyperrealism was not what I had in mind, so I fast-forwarded to avoid seeing anymore butt pimples.

Male viewers, however, would probably appreciate the final segment, "I Touch Myself, I Touch the World," which showed Karen, a pretty blonde who is "temporarily without a partner." Dr. Sommers explained that "Karen finds deep satisfaction in her own erotic self," as she fingers herself while staring at a photo of her boyfriend. As her arousal escalated, Dr. Sommers's voice began to quiver, and I wondered if he was touching himself, too.

Playboy's Secrets of Making Love . . . to the Same Person Forever is for married couples who need to put some spark into their boring and sexually stultifying relationships. (Apparently Hef made this video *after* his stroke.) Several couples openly discussed their dreadful sex lives, the men complaining that women never initiate sex and the women complaining that men never take off their baseball caps. To "add spice," the video advised bathing together, doing strip-teases, and giving sensual massages, illustrating all three to the accompaniment of "Music for Lovers," which sounded like elevator music. If couples really wanted to juice up their sex lives, they should consider asking someone else to join in. ("Honey, is the baby-sitter coming over tonight?") The only useful tip to be learned from *Secrets* was that while women hate doing it in the backseats of cars when they first meet someone, once they've been married for years the backseat becomes a big thrill. (It would have been really exciting if they had stolen the car first.)

Next I popped in *The Better Sex Videos*, an eight-part series co-narrated by Dr. Judy Seifer, a matronly sex therapist with the look of a corporate personnel director. Volume I began with several couples sharing testimonials about their troubled sex lives. Mary and Robert, married for six years, recounted how Robert first nailed Mary in his car, then just rolled off. Mary expressed disappointment as Robert graciously explained that sex for him has always been a matter of "releasing a load." Eager to improve their sex life, Robert learned to "slow down" and to develop a taste for Mary's muff. By the tape's end, Robert had become more sensitive and Mary had developed excellent fellatio skills. "There's nothing in an ejaculation that is in any way harmful to swallow—except maybe a few calories," said Dr. Seifer as Robert exploded in Mary's mouth.

My favorite couple was Bill, a pilot, and his wife, Virginia, a publishing executive. Compared to the other modestly endowed men in these videos, Bill's organ was a nuclear submarine, and for a few minutes, their office sex scene was like watching good porn. Unfortunately, it was ruined by Dr. Seifer's passion-killing narration, so I hit the mute button and supervised their desktop thrusting.

As I watched, I couldn't stop wondering where I had seen Bill before. Then it hit me: I first spotted him in one of those 970-JOIN commercials on New York's porn channel. I also remember seeing him on the "In and Out with Dick" show discussing his graduation from the Yale School of Drama (Master's in 69?), and his stint in the industry doing live sex shows in Tokyo. His credibility as a "pilot" now shot, Bill's moves suddenly seemed professionally choreographed as he landed his nose cone into Virginia's cockpit.

Volume II, *Advanced Sexual Techniques*, made me feel like a perverted med student as I studied maps of the G spot and learned about the paranometer, a machine that measures the tightness of vaginal muscles. This was demonstrated by a woman who stuffed herself with a rubber plug that was hooked up to a blinking contraption. As she flexed her muscles, it lit up like a vaginally powered pinball machine.

The next volume, *Making Sex Fun (With Games & Toys)*, featured a display of ben wa balls, two spheres that ancient

Chinese women used to slip into their vaginas to strengthen the inner muscles, and the Butterfly, a strap-on vibrator worn beneath a woman's underwear. Though the Butterfly can be used in public, the narrator warned that it does emit a slight buzz when turned on, adding, "you may not want to wear it is quiet places." I made a note never to wear one to the library, fearing that someone would tap my shoulder and say, "Excuse me, miss, could you lower the volume between your legs?"

The video also recommended that "If you keep a vibrator in your desk for dull times at the office, you can say you use it when your neck gets sore." As women stuffed themselves with variously shaped dildos and vibrators, Dr. Seifer pointed out that they are "great for travel." I pictured the customs inspector opening my bag and my having to go with either the sore neck story or telling him I was a traveling salesman.

Many of the videos recommended using these tools for women who had "problems with orgasm." Maybe this explains why I don't own one. I never thought about using machines to perk up my sex life. It's not that I'm opposed to them, I just can't imagine having a romantic encounter with an appliance that reminds me of a car phone. (Okay, maybe I'm secretly afraid I might really like them.) In the *Loving Better* series, Bob waxed Renee's bush with a giant vibrator that looked like a cross between a minivac and a shoe polisher. He barely moved, but the machine sent her into a frenzy.

My carnal knowledge only slightly improved, I skipped to the *Games & Toys* segment on bondage. "It's fun to beg for mercy," said the narrator, "but don't do anything you wouldn't do if not tied up" (that is, don't chain someone to the radiator for two days and leave him). Dr. Seifer also warned against using ropes—"they can cause burns"—and handcuffs—"It can be embarrassing if you lose the key and have to call 911."

After all this practical advice, I wanted something more esoteric. *Intimacy and Sexual Ecstasy* was hosted by Dr. Suzanne Rapley and Jonathan Robinson. Using repackaged Taoist and tantric sexual traditions, they've devised a series of exercises that increase the intensity of orgasm by delaying it. First, they started with the Kegel exercises, where you're supposed to quickly contract the P.C. muscle (puborogenous muscle) seventy-five times. This can be done anywhere, and once I heard that, I was Kegeling away. Everywhere. This exercise prepares for other techniques, like the Big Lift: "As you near climax, stop thrusting, inhale deeply, and hold your breath . . . tighten and relax the P.C. and butt muscles ten times . . . sending energy to your spine and head."

Just as I was starting to learn something—Eastern techniques like how to store sexual energy in the naval—the segment was over and the tape quickly moved to masturbatory techniques. In fact, every tape I watched covered this subject. As the doctor narrated, a guy named Gary fondled his red briefs. "Perhaps stroking yourself with your underwear on may help to slow down." "If you've never experimented with both hands, you should try it," added her co-host. I was surprised how much time these sex-ed tapes actually spent on male masturbation. I thought this was one thing every man knew how to do.

American Gigolo

Paying for My Sins

Unlike most men, who don't even buy their own underwear, most women love to shop. But the last thing a woman would think of buying is a man. Having been objectified by the male species for centuries, the thought of paying for sex seems hypocritical. Or so I thought, until a girlfriend recently confessed that hiring a call boy had become a fantasy of hers. With that in mind, I invited her over to help me penetrate the unknown world of male prostitution.

The escort services advertised on New York's porno channel—most of them with pseudo-elegant names like

Champagne Taste, Riviera, and Bon Vivant—said they provided companionship for those with "the most discriminating taste." One ad promised that it was "New York's answer to being alone." Another assumed that it would put a smile on my face. I called that one.

The guy who answered the phone had the creepiest voice I've ever heard in my life and asked what I was interested in. Having no personal preference, I relayed my friend Traci's request for a "European guy with dark hair." "We want someone to dance for us," I said nervously. When he heard the word "us," the price shot up. "It's $200 per person per hour or $275 each with a credit card, but I'll give you girls a deal for $350." I read him my credit card number and waited for someone named Rudy, who according to his "pimp" had a "really nice body." As we waited for him to show up, we had to admit this was much more exciting than ordering Chinese food.

When I opened the door, Rudy's face lit up when he saw the two of us. We both tried to keep the stupid smiles off our faces as he sat down. He was hot, sexy in that male-strippery, studly kind of way with really long black curly hair and a hunky body stuffed into jeans and cowboy boots.

This was his first trip to SoHo, as most of his calls came from uptown, "where people think differently." He was excited at the prospect of having sex with two downtown beatnik chicks until I told him I was a journalist and just wanted to ask him some questions. He looked disappointed that we weren't going to be willing "johnettes," but added provocatively, "Well, you never know what we might end up doing."

Originally from Russia, Rudy started working at Chippendale's to finance his education as a physical therapist. There, he was approached by several escort services who told him that he could "make money from women who will take you out, but you won't have to have sex if you don't want to." "I decided to do it because I was sick of waxing the hair off my body," he told us. He claimed that many men do this part-time, adding, "One guy at my agency is a dentist who moonlights."

He said his calls are from "a lot of business ladies. I don't get many calls from single women," he noted. "It's usually from people who are married. And 25 percent of my calls are from married couples. Many of the husbands want to watch while I have sex with their wives." He reported that recently he slept with the wife of a "very prominent, current U.S. senator" as the senator looked on. "The husband has a hard time keeping it up," he said. "The whole time I was doing her he kept yelling, 'So, do you like it, bitch?'"

Rudy reported that he sleeps with many high-powered women as well as those with famous husbands. "Just last week I had a judge who wanted me to pull her around by her nipple clamps. Then she wanted me to whip her. She told me it helps her job. She feels really guilty when she sends an innocent man to jail."

During the summer, his agency gets a lot of calls from German and Swedish women who want "black men with huge penises." Which led me to ask him if size was a job requirement. He nodded. "They made me show it to them before they hired me." At this point, Traci, who thought her job was to confirm everything Rudy was saying, reached down and fondled his penis through his pants. She smiled and gave me two thumbs up.

When I asked him if he ever felt humiliated in his line of work, he didn't flinch. "I love sex. And if a lady is so horny she has to pay for it, I get really turned on." Conversely, he reported that some older women like to see him two or three times before they have sex because they want "a relationship first." (Here we see a major difference between men and women. If a man is shelling out $300 an hour, the only "relationship" he wants is between his penis and her vagina.) His parents don't know what he does; nor does his girlfriend. Apparently she doesn't get suspicious when his beeper goes off at four in the morning. After forty minutes of questions, Traci started looking at her watch. "I need a massage," she announced, as Rudy pulled her onto his lap. As I tried to ask more questions, she started moaning—she and her breasts looked like they were having the time of their lives. After five minutes of this, I began to get annoyed, so I kicked Traci off and had Rudy work on my orbs. The way he expertly pleasured my nipples convinced me that physical therapy would be an excellent career move.

As I was enjoying myself, Traci put on some thumping 70s disco music and egged on Rudy to dance with shouts of "Go, baby, go!" Our John Travoltavich sprang to action, ripping off his shirt, swinging it around his head, and yelling in his Russian accent, "You girls are wild!" As we encouraged him by yelling, "Dance, Rudy, dance!" he performed a rousing but ridiculous Chippendale's routine that included floor drops, spins, and pelvic thrusts. After an hour, his agency beeped and he told them over the phone he was "putting his clothes back on." Rudy offered to stay overtime "for free," but we declined his offer as he discoed out the door. We said we'd call him in about twenty years when our husbands were impotent.

The second service I called asked me what I was looking for and gave me a menu over the phone. "We have Latins, African-Americans, Europeans, Australians, or all-American types." They all sounded delicious, so I told them to send me a "surprise grab bag."

Two hours later when they called back to tell me they had found a boy for me, I realized I had contacted the same agency as before, although the number was different. I was talking to the same creepy pimp again, who Rudy described as a "400-pound pervert."

"Are you with your girlfriend?" he wanted to know, breathing heavily.

A few minutes later, Scott arrived. He was a pretty all-American boy with blond hair, blue eyes, and a simulated preppie outfit consisting of a blue blazer, chinos, white shirt, and loafers that didn't match his Queens accent. I was told that he was twenty-three, but he confided that he was actually twenty-seven. Scott was wearing earrings in both ears and was not exuding sexuality like Rudy, so I asked him if he was gay, bi, or straight. "I'm bi," he said, following it with the yuppie-whore statement of the decade, "If someone's willing to buy, I'm willing to sell."

Scott, who said he hustles to "pay for law school," is hooked up with four agencies—two straight and two gay. "I work mostly for wealthy professionals on the Upper East Side," he said, emphasizing the word *wealthy*. "Some of these older guys just want to look at someone young and good-looking. They just want to touch you and worship your body. And unlike women, they always go down on you. A lot of these men request my type—they want a clean-looking blond who is attractive," he says, suddenly a member of the master race.

Scott got into the business after he applied at Chippendale's and was rejected. Then he met someone who suggested escort services.

Since he was being frank, I asked, "So, what do you do when you have to sleep with some lumpy old slob?"

"I close my eyes and think about paying my Visa bill," he replied. "Then I pretend I'm having sex with Richard Grieco."

Sometimes his "clients," as he referred to them, request services that he is unwilling to provide. He won't get tied up ("I like to be in control") or let guys penetrate him. He will, however, do them, if they want. Yet he did seem to worry about AIDS, and said he's never had any diseases, noting, "I always use condoms and get tested frequently." He added that many women insist on using Saran Wrap when he goes down to taste the tuna.

Since he does boys and girls, he has noticed differences. "More men than women like to play S&M games," he reports. "Most of the women just want you to make them feel attractive."

By his account, Scott figured that male escorts are not as in demand as female escorts, who represent 90 to 95 percent of the total outcall business. "Some of the wealthier men use the service once or twice a week and spend $100,000 to $200,000 a year," he claimed. The escorts earn approximately 50 percent of the fee. When I asked what he thinks about people paying for sex, he said, "Paying for sex fulfills a need people have. For them, it's a way to get what they normally can't. The only way some of them can get someone attractive is to pay for it. Besides that, it's convenient."

Rationalizing his profession, he stated, "I don't think I'm doing anything wrong. I feel sexy doing this. It's definitely an ego trip. It's kind of thrilling to get paid for it. It's like living on the edge." This sounded convincing until two minutes later when he said, "I think it's kind of sad when you have older people who have to find it by paying for it, people calling and wanting to get off." Despite this, he said his business is to "fulfill people's fantasies that they can't fulfill otherwise. We all have fantasies." And his? "To have sex with a totally straight couple and deflower the guy," he answered. And what does he hate most about his job? "Missing 'Melrose Place.'"

After Scott left, I told some of my girlfriends what I was doing. Surprisingly, everyone volunteered to come over and help me with my research. I decided to go it alone and called another service, ordering a "hot Italian sausage." They sent Joey, who had black hair, green eyes, and perfect teeth. He was so adorable he caused a tingling expansion in my groin area. I decided to question him in the nude, thus making the interview more "professional." He cheerfully agreed, then stripped. His eager attitude impressed me.

The first thing I wanted to know was what his weirdest sexual request had ever been. "I have a woman who likes her eyeballs stimulated with my tongue," he told me. "You know, the lower lids licked lightly. It almost becomes a religious experience with us." Next he told me that women wanted certain things from him that they don't get from their husbands or dates. "Women want you to be in to them, rather than in to yourself," he said. "And it may sound corny, but they want sensitivity and romance. Sexually," he pointed out, "a lot of men won't eat women out and women want that."

Joey is a happy hooker and of the three escorts seemed to enjoy his job the most. He doesn't even seem to mind jumping out of bed three or four nights a week when his beeper beckons. "I love to please," he said. "It's exciting, it's an addiction. I'll never check out of Hotel California." He claimed he also worked a full-time job as a media buyer for a Madison Avenue ad agency. Since many of his clients were career women, his preoccupying fear was being recognized by a trick when he walked into a meeting. Another downside, he said is that the escort job made it impossible for him to have a girlfriend. "If I fell in love, I couldn't subject her to this."

Another occupational hazard is "regulars" who fall in love with him. "I don't know what to say when a repeat client tells me that after she's seen me three times." I wondered how women could be in love with a man knowing he has slept with three other people that night and comes home with pubic hair in his teeth and a nasty case of crotch breath.

Joey claimed that his clients range in age from girls in their twenties to women in their thirties and forties, primarily in the fashion industry. "The women in their sixties mostly want dancing," he said. He doesn't worry at all about aging himself. "I'm good for the next ten years," he said, "then I'll become a 'walker' for another twenty." A walker is a paid escort catering to a small circle of socialite women who want a date to accompany them to black-tie social events. There is no agency for this, but walkers' names are exchanged by word of mouth.

One thing Joey mentioned that I cannot imagine men doing was making excuses for their body's imperfections. "When I see women for the first time, they apologize for their small breasts or their fat thighs," he said. When I ask him how he keeps it up for women who aren't attractive, he replied, "I try to find a redeeming quality in someone, some attractive feature—her legs, breasts, something, and I focus on that. But I get some beautiful women who just don't want to deal with assholes," he said. "They want someone to be nice to them who is not going to try to control them. Many are married," he pointed out, "merely wanting a little 'strange' while hubby is away." Confirming what the other escorts said, he noted that some of his clients have voyeuristic husbands who want to watch. "The husbands tell me they are projecting. They are having a fantasy that they are me."

The more I questioned Joey, the more excited "little Joey" became. I decided to get my money's worth and experience the thrill of the world's oldest profession first-hand. As I ordered him around ("fondle these, buster"), I realized that having someone worship you is one of life's better turn-ons. I made him pose in several compromising positions. Then I made him pleasure himself while I took a few Polaroids. Our session ended with a bang. His.

Lip Service

On Being a Cunning Linguist

Most men love oral sex. They love receiving it, that is. Giving it is another story. My experience, and that of my girlfriends, has led me to the conclusion that only half of the male population are cunnilingual enthusiasts. This statistical data is confirmed by the two-to-one ratio of men on the streets of New York who scream "Blow me!" as opposed to "Sit on my face!"

The reasons for such ambivalence toward this activity are numerous. Some men are so anxious to stick it in that they bypass cunnilingus altogether. Others are selfish and don't get much satisfaction from giving someone else pleasure.

Our culture traditionally teaches men to conquer and women to serve, so a man may be uncomfortable taking a submissive stance. Consequently, when a man is on his knees it's easier to see if he is selfish or if he has any real interest in our pleasure. It also lets us see what he would look like with a mustache.

Another often-cited excuse for lack of enthusiasm is the occasional aroma. This is perfectly understandable. I myself have put my head between a pair of legs, intending to drive someone wild with my oral skills, only to stop myself after catching one whiff of a scent closely resembling a urinal. I therefore can sympathize with someone who does not want to lick something that may at times seem like a wedge of limburger cheese with a bad toupee.

On the other hand, I salute the other 50 percent of the male population, the true oral fans. I'll never forget the first time someone dove between my legs. Unfortunately, it didn't happen until I was twenty-three years old. I was breaking in the front seat of my new car and got so excited by the tingling sensation that I accidentally hit the gearshift and plowed right into the garage door, smashing the front end. (Imagine explaining this one to the insurance adjuster.)

One orally ambidextrous boyfriend specialized in pearl diving. In fact, that's all he wanted to do. This was fine with me. I appreciated his jubilant attitude and made sure to cheer him on with shouts or "Nobody licks my monkey like you do!" After a month of this, I became tongue-whipped. (the female equivalent of pussywhipped), and even offered to do his laundry if he would come over and satisfy me.

After two months, I put a framed photo of his tongue on my desk.

One reason the sport of muff diving is not practiced more often than women would like it to be is that some men don't know how to do it. To some men, the female anatomy is still a mystery. For them, I offer a few tips. First, take the gum, cigarette, or toothpick out of your mouth. If you wear glasses, take them off so they won't get fogged up. If you are worried about feminine hygiene, spread some Tic Tacs down there.

Start by kissing her and talking to her like Barry White. Then head for the breasts. Suck those. For some women, the nipples are directly connected to the genitals. Once you've discovered the fertile crescent, locate the clitoris so you can see what you're doing. (It's the tiny pink thing on top that doesn't kiss back but really likes you.) Since every woman is different, it helps to have an inventory of techniques. Practice does help, but training on a peach would make anyone feel like a loser. Try the "silken swirl" or the "Baskin Robbins." Whatever you do, keep your tongue moving. This will only lead to voluntary reciprocation. In addition to oral moves, some women occasionally like a finger or two inserted into the love nest. A frisky nose is always welcome, as is a "Miami Vice"–stubbled chin. Refrain from inserting teeth, fists, or feet.

Avoid putting direct pressure on the little man in the canoe until it seems very aroused. Signs of escalating excitement include moaning, grunting, and threatening to commit suicide if you stop. Then head right to the love button.

Signs that she's having an orgasm range from heavy breathing to fingernails digging into your back to convulsions. If you see her eyes rolling back in her head or hear shouts of "Hallelujah!" you can be sure you did something right.

One note: Since many women are multiply orgasmic, oral sex is just the beginning of the encounter, a sort of tantalizing appetizer to the zucchini entrée. Many prefer having an orgasm by something more probing, and let's face it, not too many have eight-inch tongues.

Where to perform cunnilingus is another story. Hanging from a chandelier is a logical location. Another good place is the kitchen sink. This can have its disadvantages, however, like the time I tried it and ended up repeatedly banging my head against the toaster.

The 69 position is more awkward for women. Working out the logistics of fitting mouths over orifices and protrusions while adjusting to the rhythm is like playing a game of Naked Twister. This position further emphasizes the intimate-yet-impersonal contradictory nature of oral sex. With 69, a side-by-side position is recommended over a top-and-bottom configuration to avoid accidental death by asphyxiation, a lesson to be learned from the 400-pound woman I read about in the *Weekly World News* who suffocated her husband to death when she sat on his face.

Once the thrill of cunnilingus is gone, the after-kiss slowly approaches. It's not that the scent of our own womanhood bothers us, but smelling ourselves is a reality check. At this moment, a handshake is better than a kiss.

Hugh Hales-Tooke

Facts of Life

The Booby Trap

My Cup Runneth Over

By 1992, boob jobs were becoming the nose jobs of the 90s. Millions of women were paying up to $4,000 for a set good enough to get them an acting job in a Russ Meyer film. Male plastic surgeons got rich while their female patients got cancer. Suddenly, the breast fest came to a screeching halt. Men love tits: big ones, small ones, any one's. But especially big ones, which explains why so many women are willing to consider changing their bodies.

The relationship between women, their breasts, and the male gender is a complicated one. In the 70s, when giant breasts were not exactly trendy, I prematurely hit puberty. At age eleven and a half, growing breasts was a traumatic experience, not to mention an embarrassing one. Back then, I had no desire to have what women shell out for today. Besides clashing with my braces and Girl Scout uniform, my burgeoning womanhood and two uninvited guests arrived quite unexpectedly. I remember lying in bed one morning, staring at my new developments and wondering "Who ordered the melons?"

While most flat-chested girls my age were still skipping rope, I was being approached by strange men outside the school yard. One gave me his card and said he wanted me to pose for a "fashion" magazine called Frederick's of Hollywood. I regret now that I didn't do it.

I was the first girl in my fifth-grade class to sprout. I remember cringing when I saw my school photograph. It read "Mrs. Dietrick; Fifth Grade, the Brush School." There I was, lined up in the third row, surrounded by scrawny little girls with pigtails and glasses. Next to them, I looked ten years older and was stacked like a Playboy bunny.

By the time the fifth grade was over, the other girls in my class had still not matured. At our yearly awards ceremony, while others were winning "most reliable student" and "best math student," I won "student most likely to be felt up by boys."

I had this prepubescent notion that my mother had large breasts because she was an opera singer and it never occurred to me that I would get them myself. As mine emerged, I said to her, "I hope I don't get big jugs like yours, Mom." She matter-of-factly replied, "Don't worry, when you get older the boys will like them." What an odd thing for my mother to say. What do boys have to do with *my* breasts? I soon found out, in the backseat of a car.

Today, whenever my breasts are on display, they continue to elicit primate behavior from men. At parties, I either attract sex-offender types or guys under five foot three who insist on dancing with their noses wedged directly into my cleavage. I like to look sexy, but it's difficult to show off the merchandise and simultaneously engage a man in conversation; usually he isn't listening and his eyes are hypnotically glued to my breasts.

Some men think that a woman's IQ is inversely proportionate to the size of her breasts. They think that if a woman is bosomy, she can't possibly be intelligent, as well. On the other hand, I've seen how the sex appeal of breasts can lower a man's IQ, turning an ordinarily intelligent adult into a male bimbo (a bimboy), stuttering like an idiot at the sight of sexy cleavage.

As to who wants acquired enlargements, there are geographical differences. New Yorkers are too paranoid to rush into breast surgery. They lie on the couch, worrying about losing sensation in their nipples, ugly scars, collapsing silicone, leaking saline, and radiation treatments for cancer. Cleavage queens in L.A., on the other hand, form car pools and stop off for an operation on the way home from the mall.

Although most men like to think of themselves as connoisseurs of women's bodies, most can't tell the difference between real breasts and fake ones. But women know it's easy to detect implants: they're rounder, firmer, and they don't move. If you want to spot them on the beach, look for the ones that stick straight up in the air and don't flap to either side when a woman is on her back. Look for swimmers using them as flotation devices.

While men are busy rating our physical attributes, women are thinking that most men spend too much time evaluating our bodies. Women don't spend equal time judging male buttocks. The last thing a woman who goes through all the trouble to get beautiful new breasts wants to hear is some caveman yelling, "Hey, honey! Let's see you jiggle those rubber balloons!"

My friends with implants are now going through the same things I went through when I was eleven. They love their new additions, but say they must avoid pool halls, bars, sports arenas, and all places where men drool easily.

Another annoyance is that implants make the breasts heavier. One friend complains that she can no longer perform her twirling-the-tassels-on-the-pasties trick. Others complain about scars when the implants are inserted under the breasts rather than beneath the nipple. But as one liberal-minded male once said, "When I'm groping my girlfriend's breasts in the dark, I'm not exactly focusing on her scars." Perhaps the most disturbing side effect is that up to half of all silicone implants can solidify like rocks. One girl I know is on her second pair. She knew they had become hard when her boyfriend suggesting putting on boxing gloves so he could use them as punching bags.

Which raises the question: Are implants a quest to look

like the perfect blow-up doll just to please men, or do they represent some newfound control for women over their own bodies? Ultimately, women are doing it to please men. But first, they do it for themselves, out of a feeling of inadequacy and the desire to look better and feel more confident. On the other hand, not all men are breast-obsessed, and some prefer sexy legs or a nice butt. Men are not exactly forcing women to get the operation by hoisting them up on racks. Put simply, if we existed in a "Twilight Zone" episode where the whole planet was populated by only heterosexual women, breast implants would not exist.

The most disturbing aspect of implants is that suddenly my own breasts, which I've always loved and which I've always thought were just right, seem outdated, like last season's dress or last year's car. My natural breasts are a bit softer and not as "perfect" as my friends' new-and-improved bionic boobs.

Looking on the bright side, I might one day welcome these medical advances. Years from now, when I'm a senior citizen with saggy hooters, I'll have the option of getting a lift. Then I'll get back to wearing a 36C instead of a 36 long.

Party Etiquette

Missed Manners

For men, the ideal party is a celebration of life, puberty, and the pursuit of telephone numbers. Women, however, entertain a more complex fantasy: we go to parties hoping to see Prince Charming across a crowded room and leave him intoxicated by our charms before the stroke of midnight. But sometimes all we spot is a man dancing with underwear on his head, making gastrointestinal sounds with his armpits.

Etiquette is important. In 1922, Emily Post wrote the definitive code: "Any behavior that is discourteous or offensive to others" is considered improper. But whether at a frat-house party or a black-tie function, suitable conduct is crucial for success—particularly with members of the opposite sex. Most women, for instance, would be turned off by a man who walked up and asked, "Are those things real?"

It is always in good taste to be invited to the parties one attends, but crashing needn't be considered rude. Unless, of course, you arrive with other people and it's a sit-down dinner party. If you find out about a party you're not invited to, consider yourself a guest and go anyway! Then cheerfully introduce yourself at the door as if you were invited by a mutual friend. Once you are finished with that formality, refrain from helping yourself to pocket-size antiques or silverware.

Introductions are an essential element of good etiquette. When presenting yourself, keep it simple. Pickup lines went out with leisure suits. Offering your name is helpful. Questions such as "Do you come here often?" or "Have we met in a previous life?" will only encourage responses like "Get out of my face, you creep." Introducing your friends gives you the opportunity to present an elevated impression of yourself. Avoid elaborate or potentially embarrassing introductions. Say, "This is my friend Bob. He's a talented artist." Don't say, "This is Bob. He's the richest guy in Boston! And his nickname at school was Kielbasa Man."

Being a good conversationalist is a great social asset. Bringing up interesting topics, making snappy repartee, and dispensing flattering comments without being obsequious is always appreciated. Discussion of hemorrhoids is permissible only if the woman brings up the subject first and it is preceded by erudite ruminations on such topics as existential philosophy, thermodynamics, and the paradox of Maupassant.

Conversation with a person you have just met should be lively, constructive, and preferably amusing. Discourse that includes details about other people's operations, gossip about Connie Chung and Maury Povich, or what adorable thing you heard a five-year-old relative say may cause people to walk away from you.

Good table manners apply at parties. While using the correct fork is not required at an informal do, avoid picking your teeth with one. It is usually a good idea to separate eating from mingling, to avoid speaking with spinach stuck to your teeth and fermenting Brie breath. Also try not to pick up hors d'oeuvres when making small talk. They will quickly transform into projectile missiles in midsentence and you will be inadvertently saying it and spraying it.

Resist the temptation to chew food and display it on your tongue. This is considered bad form. Also refrain from chewing a handful of pretzels, spitting them out onto a plate, shaping the mixture into a ball, and telling others how "delicious the dip over there is."

Of course, eating pigs in a blanket, drinking killer punches, and doing the conga line eventually take their toll. Puking etiquette is always an individual and circumstantial matter. *When* to puke is usually not totally up to you, but *where* to puke is something you may have some control over. A large potted plant is always a sensible choice. The nearest fireplace is a second option when the bathroom is not available.

Bathroom behavior is an extremely delicate area. Since most people drink at parties, the one or two bathrooms suddenly become prime real estate. Consequently, it is not considered suave to cut in front of someone in line and say, "Do you, like myself, feel an urgent pressure on the inside walls of your bladder?" And it is unthinkably rude to hog precious bathroom space by using it as a make-out station or pharmacy. Worse yet, don't plug your nose and fan the air as someone exits, especially if it's the person you're interested in.

Making a favorable impression also extends to post-party etiquette. The period between the night you take someone's phone number and the time you make that follow-up call could be as short as one day or as strategically protracted as a week. If you wait more than three weeks, however, she is liable to ask "John who?" when you phone. If you call at four A.M. the night of the party, completely polluted, drooling, and slurring something like "You're sooooo pretty and nice. Can I come over?" do not be surprised if she gives you an address that turns out to be a place called Peepland, where for twenty-five cents you can party in your own private booth.

You're Fired

Take This Job and Shove It

I have been fired from every job I've ever had. Of course, it was never my fault.

The humiliation began in the Girl Scouts, the first organization I was kicked out of. This experience was a precursor of my future employment history. They said I had a "bad attitude," a concept I still have problems with. This was confusing at the time, especially considering that I thought I was showing "strong leadership qualities" by introducing the other nine-year-olds to the pleasures of smoking. From there, it's been all downhill.

After three days working one summer as a waitress, I was

fired for sitting on a customer's lap. This was also confusing—I thought the owners would have been happy to see me entertaining the clientele. My next job was at a snooty woman's clothing store, where I was caught chewing a big wad of gum— a federal offense. When my boss insisted I remove it from my mouth, I asked if I should stick it on my nose. He fired me as I put the wad on his Armani lapel.

After that job, I took various prestige jobs such as an on-the-street cigarette hander-outer (where I had to strap a big box around my neck) and a department store perfume sprayer (where I had to say, "Experience the exhilaration of autumn" eighty million times a day).

I soon learned that while getting canned from a dream job can be a depressing event, losing a job you can't believe you took in the first place can really lower your self-esteem. Those are the times you contemplate going into the garage for a bong hit on the car's exhaust pipe.

After I graduated from college and went to graduate school, I was ready to move to New York and climb the career ladder. No magazine would hire me for reasons that eluded me, so I took a job in another field to pay the rent. I was hired to work in a fashion designer's showroom showing clothes to buyers. For this job, I was required to attend EST, Werner Erhard's weekend seminars in "self-actualization." Not exactly exhibiting a gung-ho attitude about this "vocational training," I was "let go" after a week for my unwillingness to attend the "communication workshop" and become "part of the family."

A few days later, I was reading the want ads and noticed that the Pink Pussycat Boutique, an erotic novelty store in the

West Village, was advertising for "EST grads only." This is when I wondered: Are eighty hours of psychological indoctrination really necessary to sell dildos?

Eventually I found my way into the magazine business, where I discovered that adhering to strict regulations was a problem for me. During one stint as a fashion writer, my boss informed me that I dressed like a "kooky eighteen-year-old" instead of like a "professional." I took this as a compliment and said, "Professional what?" Smiling like a state trooper doing his job, she fired me.

During another job as an advertising agency copywriter, I went to the ladies' room to take a load off my mind—it's where I do my best thinking. Unfortunately, I fell asleep on the toilet while working on a deadline. Everyone was looking for me. My boss, who was on a high-fiber diet, woke me with her grunts and multiple flushings in the next stall. She canned me for "loafing on the job."

Andy Warhol once said, "There are so many people to compete with in New York City that changing your tastes to what other people *don't* want is your only hope of getting anything." Taking that thought to heart, I've contemplated selling Bibles, becoming an exterminator, or going to Apex Tech with a bunch of ex-cons to learn auto mechanics. Then I remembered that in Jack Kerouac's novel *Subterraneans* the worst thing a Beat chick or cat could do was sell out to the squares by going nine-to-five. I realized that I was a 90s Beat and that getting fired was actually good for me. It made me what I am today. Now I sit in my apartment in the middle of the day playing bongos in the nude.

IT HAPPENED TO THEM

TAMA JANOWITZ, AUTHOR

After college, I decided I would become a copywriter. I went to an ad-agency interview wearing a fox fur piece, spike-heeled boots, and a short black skirt. The execs took one look at me and my portfolio of would-be ads and hired me as an assistant art director. Even though I didn't know how to draw, my first assignment was to draw a John Wayne–type cowboy going into a bar and ordering a can of Underwood deviled ham. When I showed them the storyboard, they looked at each other and said, "When we have something for you, we'll call." Six weeks went by. One day I was asked by a woman in the office what I did exactly. I said, "Well, honestly, I sit in my office all day." She told the boss, and the next day he fired me.

TOM ROBBINS, AUTHOR

One of my duties at the *Richmond Times-Dispatch* was to edit the Earl Wilson show-business column. Every day I'd select a picture of someone Wilson mentioned. One day, without a second thought, I chose Louis Armstrong. The managing editor reprimanded me for running a photo of a person of color and told me I was never to do it again. A month later, in a feisty mood, I put in Nat King Cole. This time, I was told that if I ever ran another black person's photo, I'd be fired. Shortly after, a delicious opportunity presented itself: Sammy Davis, Jr., who was singularly despised for having recently married a blonde. I gave Sammy the nod, and just before the presses rolled I beat them to the punch and headed West.

MATT GROENING, CARTOONIST, "SIMPSONS" CREATOR

I was fourteen, working on what was basically a road gang of sullen teenagers for the County Division of Parks and Memorials in Portland, Oregon. Our job was to straighten turn-of-the-century tombstones. Once, we dug them up and stacked them to the side and then couldn't remember where they went—which almost got me fired. What did get me fired was my smart-ass attitude.

SCOTT THOMPSON, COMEDIAN, "THE KIDS IN THE HALL"

I once worked as a security guard. I was really relaxed: I'd go wandering through my rounds butt-naked and photocopy my ass. One night I fell asleep, and I was found the next morning sleeping naked in somebody's office. And then they fired me.

OZZY OSBOURNE, ROCK STAR

At seventeen I worked in a factory in Birmingham, tuning car horns. After a few weeks I was fired because I was showing up late. You see, I couldn't hear the alarm clock go off every morning because I was going deaf!

FRED SCHNEIDER, ROCK STAR, B-52'S

I got fired from my job as a waiter at a colonial-style restaurant in Athens, Georgia. They said I was "unmotivated."

JOHN WATERS, DIRECTOR

I worked in Provincetown in a clothing store called No Fish Today. I was twenty, and when girls would try on too-tight Levi's and ask, "Do you think I look good in them?" I'd just say, "Honestly, *no*." I'd also never wait on anybody. I'd just sit there and read. The owner would do a double take to try to get my attention, but I still wouldn't look up, even when there were customers. She didn't have the nerve to fire me, so she just posted the schedule one week and my name wasn't on it. I went into the store and started yelling, "What's this?" and she started shrieking, "He's insane! He's insane!" Then her husband threatened to beat me up. I guess retail wasn't for me.

Male Makeovers

Before and After

You're a guy at a party, checking out the scene. You spot a female who interests you. She's sexy beyond belief. You smile. She smiles. You visualize her naked. She cocks an eyebrow. She visualizes you dressed—in something cool. "He's good-looking," she thinks, "but those clothes look like he found them in the backseat of a garbage truck."

Since caveman times, when men wore little more than a loincloth and women told them to get a new one, women have tried to change the way men dress. Just as men have that primitive urge to watch boxing matches, women long to dress men up like Ken dolls. Girls develop crushes on stylish guys at an early age, around the same time they learn that they will forever be judged more harshly than guys on their appearance. While teenage girls consult fashion magazines and cultivate a look to attract those guys, boys are nose down in the latest issue of *Penthouse*. Accordingly, a fourteen-year-old boy's fashion knowledge is limited to the lace garter belt on Miss January. I learned this the hard way. When I was fourteen I went to the movies with a classmate who, rather maturely, said he'd "pick me up after work." He showed up in his McDonald's uniform and smelled like a large order of fries.

For many grown men, sports figures are essential style models. The typical jock outfit—baseball cap, team jacket, T-shirt, sweatpants, and Reeboks—is an ensemble that many men like. All the time. Dressing that way for Yankee Stadium or a poker game is fine, but I don't know too many women, other than former cheerleaders, who want to go to dinner with a guy dressed like their seventh-grade gym teacher. Reverse the situation—most guys wouldn't be seen at a party with a girl wearing jogging clothes.

My girlfriends agree. We're not trying to nag; we just want to be with someone we are proud to be with. Okay, we admit it, we want someone we can parade around like a prize bull at a state fair. This is why we stock our closets with a men's "house jacket." This way we can ask our date to put it on and if he says, "Why?" we just tell him, "Because we're going to a costume party."

Breaking the news to someone that he dresses like a

real zero is tricky nonetheless. You can't exactly tell a guy to pick up some style and get back to you. Since style sends out personality signals, any suggestion that he is less than dashing will be taken as an indictment of his whole existence. Makeovers, therefore, can be a risky proposition. Most women I know disguise their motives. It begins at home: magazines and catalogs are left open on the coffee table; offending clothes are "borrowed" and quietly disposed of; even more quietly, a psychological campaign is begun to instill the notion that narcissism is good.

Then you go shopping together. This, of course, is a horror. From childhood, men have been scarred by expeditions for back-to-school clothes in the company of Mom. Once in the store, every girl becomes Mom, forcing you to weather the public gaze in garments clearly made for someone else. To lessen the man's paranoia, we employ a running complimentary commentary, such as "That's really you," or "Now, that looks hot, really masculine, not the least bit fashion victimy."

Sometimes this technique has its unexpected consequences. I once flattered a boyfriend into purchasing a Gaulthier jacket. He wore it to a party that night. As he went to order drinks, I spotted our host wearing an identical jacket. When the two men saw each other, they looked horrified, like two charity-ball dowagers in the same $10,000 gown. My boyfriend was furious; we would never shop together again. His rage subsided five minutes later, when a girl approached him and stroked his lapels. Suddenly he went from dud to stud, from style virgin to fashion Frankenstein. I created a monster. He dumped me two weeks later.

The power of clothes to transform may be the reason men resist being refashioned. I've learned that wrapping a nerd in a biker jacket will not make him cool, and that draping a slob in Gaulthier will not make him sophisticated. But men don't want to reflect someone else's idea of who they should be. Nor will they bow to the expectations that a spruced-up wardrobe invites. Empirical evidence proves that a man who scratches his testicles in public will continue to do so in a $1,500 suit.

Dressing should be an adventure. Better yet, it should be an aphrodisiac. Lois Lane didn't even think of going out with Clark Kent when he looked like a nerd. But once he became Superman, donning that fabulous cape and bodysuit and showing off his many bulges, she was hooked.

The Age of Innocence

Older Women/Younger Men

For as long as I can remember, I have dated older men. While younger guys offer innocence and firm body parts, older men offer experience, wisdom, and a career, as opposed to a job at Pita-to-Go. An older guy will take you out to dinner, choose an exquisite bottle of wine, speak French or Italian to the waiter, and make interesting, illuminating conversation before he tries to get you into bed. Most younger guys are less experienced in the art of seduction. Their idea of a dinner date is bringing an overnight bag and two falafel sandwiches.

But this lack of seductive savoir faire bothers me less and

less as I find myself suddenly "the older woman" at thirty. Sometimes I wonder where all the interesting thirty- to thirty-five-year-old men are that I would like to date. (They are flirting with me as they are pushing their baby strollers down the street.)

Now I am in the role of the teacher, the coach, the one who has to watch someone go through an identity crisis. But I actually like dating someone who is so anxious and nervous that after whipping off my clothes and go-go dancing on the couch, all I have to do is point and say things like, "Go ahead, honey, it won't bite!" or "That's it, now try to get the whole thing in your mouth."

A few months ago, I started seeing someone who is eight years younger than I am. I was accused by a few people (men) of robbing the cradle. They implied that I was desperate, that I couldn't do any better, that I had lowered myself. I told them that this is not always the case. In other cultures, a male's coming-of-age often involves initiation by an older woman. Turkhana warriors of eastern Africa are encouraged to make love with adult women in the village. In the Melanesian islands, young bucks learn the ropes by making love to married women. ("Take my wife, please!") Still, our society doesn't give women who like younger men much support. Recently, I came across a fashion spread in the *New York Times Sunday Magazine* featuring clothing worn by superwaif models, none of whom looked older than twenty-two. Three out of four male models, however, had receding hairlines and matching gums—one was even carrying a cane as an accessory.

I thought about the subliminal message this spread conveyed about age and beauty, women and men. This led me to think that either life is unfair, or the fashion spread was put together by a group of middle-aged, balding men. It perpetuated the idea that older men are "distinguished" and older women are out of the picture.

When it comes to dating, the double standard is even more pronounced. When an older man goes out with a beautiful younger woman, he is met with a way-to-go virility cheer.

A woman seeing a younger man is almost always the butt of the joke. (Especially when she is a big star named Cher and falls in love with a guy who makes bagels for a living.) When Mimi Rogers, thirty-one, married Tom Cruise, twenty-five, their age gap was mentioned every time they appeared in print. Yet when forty-something Richard Gere married twenty-something Cindy Crawford, they were voted *People*'s "Most Beautiful Couple." After the fifty-something Dennis Hopper married a dancer young enough to be his daughter, the applause sign flashed. I can just imagine the comments if the roles were reversed. ("Where'd he find the hag? Jurassic Park?")

I wasn't thinking about age differences as I danced with "Junior," who I met late one night at a nightclub. I didn't know until I was sitting on his lap that he was nine years younger than I am. It didn't seem to matter—by the end of the week I was sitting on his lap every night.

At first, Junior was excited to date me and touched me with lines like "You're the best thing that's ever happened to me!" This is sweet but somehow difficult to take seriously when it's coming from someone who still lives with his parents. We spent most of our time together inside my apartment because he didn't have any money and was a little shy about meeting my friends. After two months he started complaining about being used as a boy-toy—in bed he seemed to have no objection to being a sex object, but afterward he wanted me to respect him for his mind.

There is a certain power in going out with younger men. This power, usually enjoyed by males, has to do with who controls the relationship. For most women, it's a new experience to go out with a more adoring, less dominating younger man. For once, we get to be on top.

I'm not the only one who likes this position. One thirty-five-year-old girlfriend confessed to a passionate two-month affair with a sixteen-year-old pizza boy she met behind the counter. (He had an extra-large pepperoni and delivered in less than thirty minutes.) Another thirty-seven-year-old college professor friend is dating a twenty-year-old student. "Where were these cute twenty-year-olds when I was in college?" she once asked me. In kindergarten, I told her.

Most of my guy friends think nothing of dating young cubs. One forty-year-old refers to his nineteen-year-old as his "protégé." They have a student-teacher relationship—each week they have an oral exam. A mind is a terrible thing to waste.

Although enthusiasm can make up for lack of experience, there are times when the maturity gap seems blatantly apparent. Recently, I met a guy who looked thirty-five. He was twenty-two. I made the mistake of accepting a date with him to Great Adventure. When we got there, he made me go on the Batman ride with him. I did, and spent the next ten minutes projectile vomiting. On the way home, he couldn't understand why I didn't feel like making out with him.

At a party recently, I met Jason. At first, I was oblivious to our eight-year age difference. Then I realized that I owned my own apartment and had an American Express card while he was still crashing on his friend's couch and thrilled to have a new library card. It really hit me a few weeks later when I was hanging out with a group of his friends at their apartment, sitting on a piece of foam covered by a comforter because nobody owned a bed. They talked about which characters they wanted to have sex with on "Class of '96" and what kind of vehicles they would buy if they had jobs. As I sat there trying to pay attention, it occurred to me that these guys grew up watching "Diff'rent Strokes" while I was hiding the fact that I lived through both Darrins in "Bewitched." It also made me wonder what Elizabeth Taylor and Larry Fortensky talk about.

What seems true is that the greater the age difference, the more chance the younger-man/older-woman relationship has of failing. In most cases, a five- or eight-year gap is no big deal, but more than ten years gets tricky. This is because people ask themselves different questions as they get older.

In our twenties, we are finding ourselves. We move away from our parents and make stupid mistakes, getting our asses kicked by life. We live for the moment. We party. We try different lovers on for size because we're not sure what we want, yet we want a lot, and we want it now. In our thirties, we define who we are and where our future might lead. By the time we hit thirty-five, our identity crisis has disappeared because we are too busy having a midlife crisis. At this age, women start doing facial aerobics to stop their chins from sagging and men start watching Hair Club for Men commercials, actually ordering the brochure on hairweaves. When we hit our forties, we may have achieved financial success, but we spend our nights sitting in our nice houses worrying about how old we are. In our fifties, we stop worrying about aging because we already have. By the time we are in our sixties, we have decided to live it up. Theoretically, this is the time we should go out with twenty-two-year-olds, who are also living for the moment.

What evens out these chronological inequities is the fact that older women and younger men have something unique to give each other. Older women offer experience, guidance, and comfort; younger men offer innovation and playfulness. They also have extra time to spend hanging out and feeding us grapes while they massage our feet. This is the essential paradox: An older woman may mother a younger guy, but he ends up babying her more than an older man ever would.

But best of all, women over thirty have hit their sexual peak, making them compatible with sex-craved men in their early twenties. While a man's testosterone level drops as he gets older, a woman's hormones begin to rage. With this arrangement, men get a chance to learn the lessons of love while women get a chance to be the premature ejaculators.

Adult Education

Ten Tips for Dating Older Women

Don't arrive for your date on a skateboard.

Don't sign a thirty-five-year-old's birthday card with "Only ten years till menopause!"

Don't say, "Age before beauty" as she exits the elevator, even if she is only twenty-nine.

Don't ask, "How did you get to be so good in bed? You must have really been around."

Don't keep referring to her as Mrs. Robinson.

Don't remind her she is aging by giving her a gift certificate to a varicose veins treatment center.

Don't rub it in by saying, "Boy, I bet that biological time clock of yours really needs rewinding!"

Don't say, "You're a high-mileage chick, but I love women with experience."

Don't tell her she reminds you of your mother.

Do ask her, "May I breast feed?"

The Wild Girls Club

Girl Talk

Part Deux

It's a sultry evening in sin city as another meeting of the Wild Girls Club convenes. It's a girls-only, no-men-allowed scene where any males who attempt to enter will be promptly ejected, rejected, and/or castrated.

Unlike Robert Bly's men's movement, we don't need to get in touch with our feelings by dancing around in a circle on our tiptoes, banging on drums, or hugging trees.

Tonight was PMS night, an evening that no man in his right mind would want to attend, yet many begged to. When I told my male friends that twenty wild women were assembling, they immediately tried to invite themselves over.

"What goes on at those things?" asked one. "Is it a bunch of girls sitting around in lingerie doing each other's hair?" asked another. A third envisioned us all trying on clothes together, running around half-naked in teddies and marabou heels. One virgin thought we exchanged recipes. Someone else thought we listened to Tori Amos and k. d. lang while using a speculum to look at each other's cervixes. Most envisioned either a pornographic pajama party or a haremlike environment filled with hot and horny nymphos deprived of men for months.

As my cohostess and I mixed margaritas and plastered the walls of her loft with *Playgirl* pictorials of naked men with tattoos on their butts, we talked about how disgusting it was that men reduce women to sexual objects. Then we talked about good places to meet guys (parties, art openings) and bad places (while hitchhiking, at VD clinics.)

I can't reveal everything we talk about, but I can say that our club is the female equivalent of men's poker night. But instead of playing a game and talking a little, we talk too much, bonding and bitching about the boys. As we waited for the other babes to show up, we wondered what twenty men would talk about if they were all together. We figured that twenty heteros would probably talk about baseball, boobs, and the guy in Virginia whose wife cut his penis off. Twenty gay men would probably sit around in lingerie and do each other's hair.

When our pussy posse arrived, we began by discussing deconstruction, the perplexities of the bicameral mind, and quantum theory. Then we moved into more difficult topics like sex with strangers and strange sex: armpit fetishes (maschalophilous); getting turned on by mannequins (agalmatophilia); and arousal from being fondled in a crowd (greegomulcia).

As the margaritas kicked in, the truth poured out. It was time for our traditional kiss-and-tell "ho of the month" segment, a requirement at each meeting, where everyone confesses their juiciest sex tale. One girl slept with an MTV personality who she reported had "an amazing body and an amazingly small penis." Another slept with a prominent art gallery owner who promised her a "big show." He showed her something big in his pants, but a month later his gallery closed. Somebody else said she made out with a bleached cyber-rock star who "kissed like a meat grinder." Someone else told her story of meeting Warren Beatty (pre–Annette Benning). They met at a nightclub and afterward he dropped her off. Then he sat in his car, called her on his car phone from below, and said, "Lift your nightgown through the window and show me your pussy." He went up to her apartment, took her clothes off, kept his on, and told her "I haven't seen a body like this in years." Then he asked if she'd ever been fisted. This story was rivaled by the girl whose father was a former U.S. senator who told us she once gave a blowjob to a cute Secret Service agent in a security booth at the White House. She told us she plans on servicing the entire U.S. military next.

A discussion of dating trends for the 90s ensued. We all agreed that in the 80s, men faked sensitivity to get us into bed. They acted like they were kind, caring Gloria Steinem fans and pretended to respect us. In the 90s the technique is to combine what they learned from the 80s with pretending they want a relationship. "Now men tell you they want a girlfriend and act like they have no problem being monogamous," said one girl. "But I still end up getting humped and dumped." We concluded that women want to find one man to satisfy their many needs while men want many women to satisfy their one need.

An interesting thing happens when women get together. Suddenly, we don't care what men think of us. We don't worry if our conversation seems unattractive and unfeminine. We say what we really think. We stop worrying whether or not we are being man-pleasing. Suddenly, we are less demure, more outspoken, and much louder. We like acting unladylike and swearing like a bunch of teamsters because we know if we acted like this in front of men they would run for the hills. We know if we slapped each other on the back and yelled things like "You slutty roadwhore, smell my finger!" our only dates would be with porn actors or deaf guys.

In honor of PMS night, we started the "I hate it, I love it" portion of the evening.

One girl screamed, "I hate guys who yell things when I'm on my bike like 'Hey, honey, can you ride my face like that?'"

Someone else said, "I love holding my boyfriend's penis when he's urinating."

A third said, "I hate it when I'm getting excited and my boyfriend starts smacking me real hard on the ass."

"I love that," said another.

A fourth said she hates Don Juannabes who try to score on

the first date. "One unsmooth operator pulled me down on the couch and said, 'Come on, baby, let's get it on.' He was serious. When I laughed in his face, he told me he was trying to be like Barry White."

" 'Let's Get It On' was sung by Marvin Gaye," someone else pointed out.

Someone else said she would love to go out with someone who treated her nicely and suggested we start a charm school for American men and "invite Italian and French guys as guest speakers."

Another girl said, "One guy took me out for the first time and after twenty minutes told me he had someone he'd like me to meet; he pulled my hand under the table and put it on his penis."

Somebody else said, "I love a man with a huge sausage who can put a lampshade on his head *and* say something brilliant."

We gave her another drink.

Breaking from our gabfest, we dirty-danced to Tom Jones songs. Then one wild woman took matters into her own hands and whipped out "Mr. Satisfier," a foot-long dildo with "a veined surface for increased stimulation." Everyone applauded. Then she mounted another club member and had mock doggy-style sex as we shouted the most inept seduction lines we'd every heard. "C'mon, little lady, say hello to Big Bob!" or "Oh baby, lemme in there—my scabs are all healed."

After the performance, the grievance committee took the floor. One entertainment lawyer complained about the men she meets who become competitive after discovering how successful she is. Someone else launched into a heated monologue about how men think they have all the power and want to control women. Another girl said, "They want an arm trophy who will be their personal slave." The consensus was that many men want a women to be inferior to them in some way—except, of course, in the looks department. Then someone added, "A lot of guys think they deserve a supermodel, particularly the ones who look like a drooling Danny De Vito."

Three hours and five rounds of margaritas later, the discussion turned back to love and sex. "I know that most guys think sex is nothing more than a good workout," one of the girls said. "But it's emotional for me. I get attached to anything that penetrates my vagina." We kept Mr. Satisfier away from her.

Suddenly there was knock at the door. We looked through the peephole and saw a man. It was somebody's curious boyfriend, gate crashing. Everyone screamed not to let him in. We took a vote and decided to go against our usually strict door policy and let him enter at his own risk. Then we depanted the victim and forced him into pantyhose. Next we gave him a twenty-girl massage. Then we put a rooster hat on his head and made him be our mascot, "Rooster Boy." He loved it so much he asked if he could come back next year.

Silvia Otte

The
Determinator

Answers to Probing Questions from the Male Room

My girlfriend complains that I stare way too hard at other women when I'm with her. But I can't help it. Any suggestions? T.L. (New York, NY)

Women find it insulting when you leer so hard at other bootie that you start to salivate. Be respectful of her feelings by practicing a little self-control when you're together. If you have a tough time curbing yourself, you can always resort to wearing an eye patch, safety goggles, horse blinders, or a welding mask.

What would a girl think about receiving a vibrator as a gift? B.F. (Portland, OR)

Some will think a vibrator is rude, crude, and unsensuous, while others will consider it a thoughtful gift. The only drawback I see here is that she might fall in love with the vibrator and dump you.

My girlfriend likes to have sex five times a day. Is this normal? D.F. (Milwaukee, WI)

I don't know what normal is, but consider yourself lucky. Most women I know don't have time to do it five times a day. If we were able to do it that often, we'd be too exhausted to do anything else and would probably have a hard time walking.

How do I approach a woman I want to meet who's standing in line at the bank? A.C. (Mountain View, CA)

Pickup lines these days seem forced, so the key is to be natural. Approaching a woman after she has used the cash machine might make her uptight, especially if she has just withdrawn a large sum of money and lives in New York. Standing next to someone in line is another story. You might want to make some comment about bank inefficiency—anything to start the conversation. Continue only if she seems interested. We like it when a guy we like tries to talk to us; however, we find it annoying when we are not interested and he fails to get the hint. She is not interested if she ignores you. Look for signals from her like flirtatious eye contact, uncontrollable smiling, or quivering lips. If she responds, keep the conversation going, and don't get nervous or you'll blurt out something idiotic. Most important, try not to keep looking down at your pants to see if your erection is showing.

What sexual position does a woman enjoy most? B.B. (Washington, DC)

This is an individual matter and ranges from those who prefer the old missionary position to those who like being suspended from a chandelier. However, the majority of women say that the woman-on-top, man-on-bottom position is a good one. Anatomically speaking, the friction is right. For a variation on this, have her bend her legs in the Easy Rider position and then give it full throttle.

Lately, I've been thinking about asking my girlfriend if she'd like to have phone sex with me. Will she think I'm a pervert? B.T. (Baltimore, MD)

I see nothing wrong with phone sex. It's the way of the 90s. And it's more germ-free than just about any other kind of sex you can have. In fact, it could be entertaining. Just make sure you don't put her on hold too long or ejaculate all over the speakerphone.

I live in a small town and am considered the town weirdo. I don't fit in and have no friends. Meeting a girl seems hopeless. Is there anything I can do to change the situation? S.T. (Liano, TX)

Get the weirdo radar going by emphasizing your differences. If people think your hair or clothes are strange, wear them like a neon sign. Soon you'll start attracting others just like yourself. Before you know it, you'll have formed your own subculture and town underground. Eventually you'll become a cult leader like Reverend Moon or Charles Manson. If all else fails, move to New York.

I'm confused. I thought women liked compliments, but when I give them to women on the street, they tell me to get lost. S.W. (New York, NY)

Screaming "Nice tits!" to a strange woman walking down the street is not exactly a compliment. This is because women can't get enough compliments from men they know and like. The problem occurs when guys like to pay tribute to women you don't know—those tributes usually involve an assessment of one or more of our body parts. In such instances, a look of admiration is more than enough. Save your words for women you already know.

I'm a terrible dancer and my girlfriend always tries to get me to dance whenever we go out to clubs. What should I do? M.M. (Athens, GA)

Learn to dance. We want to dance with you rather than have you crushing our toes. And we don't want to dance with another girl while you watch. It's a turn-on when a guy can move. If you are a spaz or can't find the rhythm, watch "Soul Train" and practice a few moves.

How many dates should I have before I try to get a girl to do the wild thing? M.S. (Fresh Meadows, NY)

It's usually a good idea to be cool on the first date. Let her give you the signals, and usually by the third date you'll know if you will be getting any. Don't be anxious; your testicles are not going to explode. If you do move in and she resists, don't persist. A buildup of tension at first is exciting. Whatever you do, don't grab her and say, "You know you want it," "Don't be so uptight," or "What are you, a lesbo?"

What is the difference between male and female fantasies? P.A. (Bar Harbor, ME)

There are usually more people involved in men's fantasies. Women's tend to be more one-on-one, although we do enjoy the occasional two-guy, one-girl threesome twin-male-model scenario.

Of course, fantasies vary widely, but I'd say that

women's tend more toward the romantic while men's are more impersonal. Also, men seem to require additional support materials, such as *Juggs* magazine or the *Sports Illustrated* swimsuit issue.

How can one be mysterious without being alienating? C.C. (Wellesley, MA)

It sounds like you want to be weird and popular at the same time. It won't work. If you're spending so much time worrying about being mysterious, then you're probably not. If you're worrying about alienating people, you probably are. If you want to be mysterious, get a personality. Mysterious people are mysterious because they are interesting to others who feel alienated because they can't figure them out.

There are certain ways a woman can protect herself from being date-raped. But is there any way I can protect myself from being accused of raping someone, especially if it is not true. I don't want to be like William Kennedy Smith. A.L. (Chicago, IL)

If you are this worried about being accused, your behavior is probably borderline. Here are some basic guidelines: You are pushing it if on the first date you rub your boner against your date's groin or say things like, "I want to be inside you." When in doubt, keep it in your pants. To ensure that you don't rape anyone, you should wear three pairs of underwear and a jockstrap. This will decrease your penile sensitivity in case you get too excited. If you are still paranoid, try taping your penis to your leg with masking tape.

My girlfriend loves just about everything to do with getting spanked. But I'd like her to spank me. How should I bring it up? Sore Hands (London, England)

This is not an uncommon fantasy, so don't be afraid to speak up. Try telling her you've been a bad boy and you need a good spanking. If this doesn't work, take a Magic Marker, write "SPANK ME" on your bare butt, and bend over.

There's a girl at the gym I'm interested in who I'm almost positive likes me, too. How do I start talking to her? F.A. (Crystal, MN)

First of all, don't try to pick her up while she's sitting on the inner-thigh machine with her legs spread apart. Also, don't approach her when she's lying on her back on the gluteus machine and your package is positioned in her face at direct eye level. Refrain from starting the conversation with "You know, I have equipment that would really give you a good workout!" The best approach is to say hello and ask her if she's ever taken the yoga class the gym offers, showing her how spiritually enlightened you are.

Do you think it's possible to fall in love with someone you met from a one-night stand? Y.R. (Nyack, NY)

It's certainly possible, but it really depends on whether you sleep with someone because you want to get laid or because you want to begin a relationship. It also depends on whether the other person left immediately afterward. (This is called a "half-nighter.") People who are into one-nighters usually don't stay long enough to find out your last name, let alone fall in love with you.

I am a thirty-year-old male and have noticed that when little kids sit on my lap, I get an erection. Am I a pervert? B.L. (Chicago, IL)

When a thirty-year-old man gets aroused by five-year-olds, yes, he is a pervert. If he actually has any form of sex with them, he is a child molester. Keep the kiddies off your lap, and whatever you do, don't get a job as Santa Claus or go over to Michael Jackson's house.

Do women find men's penises attractive? J.B. (West Pittston, PA)

When women find a man attractive, his penis can be extremely exciting and erotic. On the other hand, if we find someone repulsive, we think it's the ugliest thing on earth. Women like watching them transform from soft to hard. And yes, size does matter. If it's too big, it can hurt. If it's too small, we can't feel it. But for those a little on the small side, a huge tongue will compensate.

What would a woman think of finding a stuffed animal in a man's bedroom? J.T. (London, England)

She would think it was cute and sweet. She would think it was a boyish touch, a remembrance of childhood. She would think about how all men are little boys deep down. She would think about how men like to be babied. However, she would think it was strange if he talked to it and said things like "Nobody understands me like you do, Teddy."

My boyfriend says he really likes it when I shave my pubic hair, but it itches when it grows out. Can you tell me why he seems to like this so much? J.S. (New York, NY)

You don't have to shave it every day, but sometimes

men want to see what's "down there." They enjoy the stimulating view and like inspecting what's underneath the "crotch 'fro." Shaving comes in especially handy after a guy's had two six packs and can't find his own organ, let alone yours.

What's the fastest way to deglamorize oneself? C.C. (Wellesley, MA)

I have no idea why you want to do this, considering that people spend millions of dollars a year trying to look glamorous. But, anyway, start by eating lots of greasy foods so you'll get loads of pimples. Then, consume tons of prunes, beans, and apricots so you'll be uncontrollably flatulent. Next, don't bathe, comb your hair, or use deodorant for days. This should get you started.

I like to have my anus massaged. Does this mean I'm gay? D.K. (Dearborn, MI)

Not necessarily. Of course it depends on who is massaging it. If it's a woman, you are straight; if it's a man, you are gay. If it's a hermaphrodite, you are bi. So go ahead, enjoy your orifice!

I'm turned on by women who weigh over 300 pounds. Am I the only guy with this particular obsession? L.P. (San Diego, CA)

You aren't the only chubby chaser who believes that "the bigger the cushion, the better the pushin'." Luckily for you there is NAAFA (National Association to Advance Fat Acceptance) in Sacramento, California, and the MOR-2-Luv dating service in L.A. If you can't find anyone here, try picking up extra-large ladies by hanging out at Big &

Tall shops, fast-food restaurants, Baskin-Robbin's, or hog-calling contests.

How does alcohol affect sexual performance? C.S. (Tucson, AZ)

Alcohol may increase sexual desire, but too much may decrease genital sensitivity, reducing your organ to dead meat. Drinking too much may also cause erectile problems resulting in either premature ejaculation or no ejaculation at all. The worst drawback, however, is increased difficulty in finding the hole and the tendency to repeatedly ask if it's in there.

How do I make the first move once a girl has made it clear she wants to sleep with me? M.T. (Monroe, LA)

The art of seduction is a subtle one unless, of course, you are both completely loaded—then neither of you will be able to tell the difference. The key is to make her feel comfortable and desirable. Tell her she's beautiful. Hug her. Kiss her. Be sweet. Above all, don't say, "I haven't been laid in weeks and I'm really horny."

My lover makes too much noise and talks too much during sex. What should I do? Y.B. (Vail, CO)

Tell the person that your neighbors have been complaining. If that gets no results, suggest oral sex. If your lover still doesn't get the hint, try wearing ear muffs to bed.

Why do women take so long to get ready to go out? L.K. (Oakland, CA)

Most men judge women on their appearance, so it's true that part of us wants to look good for you. But we also want to look good for ourselves. We enjoy the ritual of putting on lipstick, painting on eyeliner, and getting our hair just right. Considering that all great works of art take time to compose, it's remarkable that in only minutes we can bring all that inner beauty to the surface.

Will women like me even if I don't make much money? P.D. (Seattle, WA)

It depends on how good-looking you are. If you are incredibly handsome and well endowed, money is not so important. The uglier you are, the more money you should have. If you have no money, you could always try going out with older women who don't need it. You could be like Elizabeth Taylor and her construction-worker husband. Or Cher and the bagel maker. Not all women are materialistic. Try to meet New Age chicks who don't care about money (like Peace Corps volunteers, horny ex-nuns, or recently released prisoners).

If I'm dating a girl and she comes over to my house, would she think I was being too forward if I had condoms on hand? J.L. (North Hollywood, CA)

Having condoms available is always a smart idea. It makes sense to have your own supply. It shows that you are responsible (or a sexaholic). If, however, you stock an assortment by the case, she may get suspicious.

Why do women want heterosexual men to be more like homosexual men? C.M. (Washington, D.C.)

If a straight man is attracted to a woman, he finds it hard to be "just friends" with her. It's difficult to become too close to a guy if either one of you is attracted to the other.

Gay men like us because they like us, and there's no sexual tension. Gay men treat us more equally; they too have been treated unfairly. They don't try to boss us around. And they don't restrict our behavior; we can act wild without being judged. Besides, we can try on each other's clothes and go out and pick up guys together.

Why do women go in pairs to the ladies' room? T.K. (Santa Fe, NM)

To talk about you. This is a place where women congregate to discuss men—ladies' rooms are official man-talk headquarters. If you're paranoid, you should be; you are being discussed.

My girlfriend says the only way she gets satisfied is when she gets on top. What's the deal? L.T. (Beloit, WI)

This is common. One reason some older women have never had an orgasm in forty years of marriage is because their husbands wouldn't let them get on top. You should welcome this position because all you have to do is lie there and watch her groan.

What are sexy things to say to a woman in bed? F.H. (Metuchen, NJ)

There is a fine line between sexy and disgusting—and it varies with every woman. During sex you can say anything from "You're incredibly sexy" to "You look so beautiful" to "You're driving me crazy." Don't say, "You make me drip." After sex, say something like, "I could make love with you every night for the rest of my life!" Prevent yourself from blurting out, "You were better than all of the prostitutes I've paid for!"

I'm nineteen years old and have only slept with one woman. I'm nervous about being alone with a woman as well as worried about contracting AIDS. Am I dysfunctional or just cautious? E.B. (Reading, PA)

Neither, these are legitimate fears. To learn how to be intimate with a woman, you need to get to know one. Once you feel comfortable with someone, you will want to try kissing, petting, and dry humping, the new sex trend of the paranoid 90s. You also might want to find another woman who might teach you a thing or two. Or you may discover you prefer men. If this is not the case, you might consider buying a sheep.

Lately, my girlfriend has been jamming her finger up my butt real hard during sex. I know that some people like being stimulated in this area, but I'm really not into it, even if it's done lightly. M.J. (Greenwich, CT)

Communicating what you like and don't like in bed is crucial to satisfying sex. Tell her exactly what you think. Tell her she hurt your butt last time. If this doesn't work, tell her you hate picking her Lee Press-On Nails off your 'roids.

Is it true that masturbation makes your penis smaller? T.B. (Alexandria, VA)

This is a frequently asked question, leading me to believe that there are a lot of guys out there having fun with themselves. Masturbation is a healthy and natural release of tension, not to mention good exercise. It will not make your penis smaller—quite the contrary, it will actually improve your growth. Increase your masturbation to five times a day for fifteen minutes, three of those using a vacuum cleaner. Try Mom's Hoover or a Sears wet/dry vac.

I'm twenty-two and still a virgin. I'm dying to have sex but too embarrassed to admit my inexperience. What should I do? J.L. (Hartford, CT)

Don't feel embarrassed if you are still a virgin. You are not alone. A much larger percentage of people are virgins these days because there are more reasons than ever not to have sex. Don't tell anyone. Just find a willing girl more experienced than you and tell her you want to be dominated. Act like you really want her to "do you" and she won't notice the difference. If this doesn't work out, you might want to consider joining the priesthood.

What kind of underwear do women find attractive? S.S. (Chicago, IL)

Whatever the style, if you feel silly wearing it, you probably shouldn't. Women have varying tastes—some even find jockstraps sexy. Most boxers and briefs are fine as long as they don't have giant stains on them. For extra excitement you could always order a pair of easy-off underwear from Frederick's of Hollywood, which tear off with a quick tug so you don't have to waste valuable time struggling to get them down to your ankles. Stay away from those tacky thongs unless you want the Chippendales/Brazilian-playboy look.

I'm really attracted to a gorgeous woman who lives in my apartment building. She has even implied that she wants to have sex with me. The only problem is that she is married. What should I do? E.N. (Brooklyn, NY)

You're better off keeping this a fantasy. Going out with married women can be dangerous. Unless you don't mind being beaten up by her husband or are built like Arnold Schwarzenegger, don't risk it.

Will women be turned off by me if I reveal to them that I am in therapy? D.L. (Los Angeles, CA)

It depends on what kind of therapy you are in. If you are a compulsive obsessive with a cleaning disorder, that's okay, because we know you will have a clean apartment and maybe we can get you to clean ours. However, if you have a problem with, say, bestiality, it may be a turnoff.

Jim Radakovich

Interviews of Men with Penises

Joe Pesci
The *Goodfella* on Women, Sex, and Boxer Shorts

Do people think you're a violent person?
Yes, often.

But you're not, right?
Mmmm . . . [grabs my neck in mock strangulation]

Have you ever played a nice guy?
I think all the guys I play are nice. I don't look at anybody as really bad—I think we've all done bad things in our lives. People have two sides. If somebody's just blah as a person, period, that's all you're going to get. But if someone is very, very nice, wonderful, and bubbly, watch out for the other side.

Have you ever been arrested?
Not for anything serious.

Where are you from?
I was born in Newark, New Jersey, and went to school in Belleville. After that, I moved up to the Bronx; that's where I got my street education. I still live in New Jersey. I have a house on the water.

What were you like as a kid?
I was different from most kids. I was busy studying my music, my lines, my scripts. I wasn't out there playing baseball.

Did you ever get beat up?
I had my share of beatings, but I gave a few, too. I was never the toughest kid in the neighborhood, that's for sure.

Did you have to work any dumb jobs to support yourself as an actor?

A million. I was a mailman, a mail clerk, than I worked as a mail handler, unloading the trucks for the post office. I was a produce manager at a market. I worked for an answering service. Listen, nobody knows what they're doing until they gain some kind of recognition doing it.

How did you start working with Martin Scorcese?

I didn't just parachute from Butte, Montana, into an acting career. I've been an actor since I was five. I did big musicals first, then I did television. Then I had a singing career for a long time. I sang jazz-blues and played the guitar. I made my first film in 1970. It was called *Death Collector*. I cowrote it with the director, and he gave me a costarring role. It was like a New Jersey *Mean Streets*. After that I quit for a while because I hated the business end of show business. De Niro saw the movie and found me in the Bronx, where I was running a restaurant. I told him I had given up acting. Then he brought Scorcese to see me to talk about a part in *Raging Bull*. The part [Jake LaMotta's brother] was small originally but got bigger and bigger.

What did you think when you won the Academy Award for *Goodfellas*?

I thought they made a mistake. I couldn't believe it. I wasn't prepared.

So you didn't write a speech?

I would never do that to myself. It's gotta be a terrible thing to hang up your tuxedo at night when no one's looking and take the speech out of your pocket.

Where did you put the statue?

Up here [points to his butt]. Some girl told me I should put a vibrator in it and let her use it. But seriously, I gave it to my mother. She gets all the awards.

Who was the babe you took to the awards?

That was my wife. Do you think I went to an escort service?

What kind of women do you find attractive?

Everyone is attracted to beauty first—a beautiful face, a great body. Then the real stuff starts to come out. A really sexy woman is sexy from the inside. She exudes sex. Some people are just hot like that, you know. I also like women who have a real love of life, who are not afraid of anything. I hate women who use men. I hate men who use women. I like being nice to women, understanding them, digging them. This is my third wife. But there were long intervals in between. She's twenty-four and studying singing. I like younger women—they perk me up. I like older women, too. They know so much.

Are you horny?

What kind of interview is this? It depends on when you ask me. Right now, I'm okay.

Do you think that Italians make the best lovers?

I don't think that, I *know* that. I think Italians are romantic. I'm romantic. Life is romantic.

So you have *la passione*?

I think I have some of that Mediterranean heat inside of me.

You don't mind questions like that?

Not even a little bit. As a matter of fact, these are the best questions you've asked.

Would you ever do a nude scene?

It depends on the situation. First of all, I don't have a Sylvestor Stallone body. But if it was in good taste and there was a good reason for it, I wouldn't hesitate to take my clothes off.

What do you do for fun?

I love to play golf, but if you had asked me that ten years ago, I would have made your face red.

What kind of underwear do you wear?

I used to wear boxers. Now I wear Jockey briefs.

Do you hang out with other actors?

Bobby De Niro and I are close friends. And Chris Walken. I have a lot of superstar friends. Like Mikhail Baryshnikov and Liza Minnelli. I'm lucky to have a group of such talented friends.

What advice would you give to a young actor just starting out?

Just do it. Those who chase fame or money are in trouble. You have to approach it artistically rather than commercially. If you want to act, act. If you want to sing, sing. You don't have to be Frank Sinatra.

Is there anything that makes your blood boil?

A zillion things. It's better to admit it when you're hot-blooded. At least you're never boring. When I'm not working, I bust out; I'm loaded with energy, anger, everything else.

How have you chosen your roles?

No one comes to you in the beginning. Now they do. I always knew which ones I wanted, which ones I didn't, which ones I could do something with. My wish is to get a good script, story, director, and actors. If you get a great director, then you're basically set.

Scorcese, for instance. He's good because he knows every detail about the characters—how they live, how they speak, what their houses look like.

Exactly. He doesn't rely on story as much as on the characters and their environment. He picks the right people and captures every detail, right down to how they cut the onions.

Are you a regular guy? Would you put yourself in that category?

No, I think regular guys are idiots. I think I'm better than regular.

Norman Mailer
America's Literary Lion Still Roars

You're sixty-eight. You wrote your first novel at twenty-five. How has the writing process changed?

The anxiety changes.

How is the process of acting and writing similar?

Just as an actor plays certain roles, I tend to project myself into the role of the character who is speaking. Just as actors can become people onstage they would never get near in life, writers can write dialogue for characters they really shouldn't be able to.

Your book [*Harlot's Ghost*] is about a CIA agent. Did you ever want to be a spy?

There's a joke about the prostitute who is asked why she got into prostitution and she says, "Just lucky, I guess." I've always been fascinated by the CIA. It has occupied my mind for thirty years. It's always there, this great mysterious presence. It's like being married. In this case, you're married to America and you're living in her house, and after a while someone tells you there's a ghost in the house. It's a very important ghost, but we never see her.

I get my best ideas when I'm sitting on the throne. How about you?

That's almost a rule of thumb. You always get the best ideas when there's no pencil around.

Why did it take you seven years to write this book?

I lived with it for seven years, but I deserted it for a period when I made the movie *Tough Guys Don't Dance*. When I went back to it, it was like going back to a wife. It's a relationship. But there's nothing sexual about writing—it's probably counterproductive toward sex.

Have you ever been to a whorehouse?

Next you'll ask me where. When I was a kid that was one of the big things you had to do. You weren't a man until you had gone to a whorehouse.

You have a very fertile imagination. What do you think about when you are masturbating?

What!? [laughs, looks at me as if I'm nuts]

Do you think the repressive morality of the 50s has resurged in the 90s?

It's very different from the 50s. In the 50s you had a morality arching overhead, a sort of umbrella morality that was very strict. But under it people were rebelling all over the place. Today it's the exact opposite. It isn't as if the crackdown is coming from the top at all, it's coming from within each person. People are afraid of sex now. In a way it's medieval; in the Middle Ages, if a woman got pregnant, her chances of dying in childbirth were very high. Anytime a woman met her lover she might also be meeting her angel of death. I think some of that element is present again.

What do you think of the so-called new censorship?

Censorship will not be the lead horse of repression. If we get into a totalitarian condition, which I think would happen only if we had a terrible depression, and things start busting loose all over and martial law is necessary, if you start having prison camps, in effect, to keep unruly people in place, at that point you might find censorship coming in.

A recent survey of college students revealed that about one-third described themselves as "open-minded." Do you find that depressing?

I think forty years ago, in the 1950s, 75 percent of people would have said they were open-minded, and they weren't at all. It could indicate that we're in a prefascistic state or that they want authority, they don't want questions, or it can mean that people are getting more self-evaluative and closer to what they really are. I think that one-third is an accurate answer at any time in any population. If you can find a third of the people open-minded, that's extraordinary. Most people are not.

Do you think kids in the twentysomething generation, who read less and watch TV more, are less articulate?

I think it's created that style of speech that's abominable: three words, three dots. "Well, you know . . ." Pause. "Like, I mean . . ." and so on. That comes from television, which is always interrupting. Television is coitus interruptus brought into aesthetics. After a while kids who grew up on it are unaccustomed to carrying a thought through. The idea that you can concentrate for more than twelve minutes means there's something wrong with you, man.

That's why kids aren't writing thousand-page novels like you—

I'm not worried about people not writing them, I'm worried about whether they're not going to be reading them.

You've been married six times. How do you explain your sex appeal to women?

[chuckles] Oh, God. "I'm innocent," said the man condemned. I think any man who has a little success with his profession is attractive to women in his circle. There's nothing mysterious about it. Henry Kissinger once was asked, "Why are you so attractive to women, Mr. Kissinger?" and he said, "Power is the ultimate aphrodisiac." I think the will to power is probably, in technological terms, more powerful than the sex drive.

Are you as interested in sex as you were, say, forty years ago?

Well, I'd like to think I'm still a fraction of that state forty years ago.

What advice would you give to a young writer starting out?

If you tell yourself you're going to write the next day, write the next day. No matter what comes up, write. I think what happens is you set up a contract with your unconscious. Your unconscious prepares the words. When you don't do that, all the material sits around your brain and starts to smolder. We're the manager of the artist in ourselves.

You've had flattering as well as horrible things written about you—

Madame de Staël was in the French court of Louis XVI. It was said that Madame de Staël threw her friends into the pond for the pleasure of fishing them out. That's the media. The media loves nothing better than to take some celebrity and throw him into the pool and drown him and, as he's about to go down for the third time, pull him up again. It loves falls, and it loves people to regain position. It can't deal with anything in between.

How do you handle people who insult you to your face?

I have about ten remarks that are useful in any number of situations. For instance, when I feel someone invading my turf, I say, "Kidding is kidding, but get your ass off my pillow" or "Once a philosopher, twice a pervert." I rarely find myself in a situation where one out of the ten won't work.

Tom Jones
Genius of Gyration

How old were you when you first started singing and the girls went crazy?

I started in Wales when I was a teenager. My first band was called the Senators, but we changed it to the Playboys.

And did you shake your bootie?

Oh yeah. But it was the voice first that got the women excited.

Where did you come up with the sexy moves?

Elvis Presley. I liked what I saw. Performers have to *express* themselves. They don't need a lot of movement, but they need to *ooze* chemistry. I knew I could *gush* like that.

When you first met Elvis in 1965, what did he say?

He thought I was black when he heard "What's New, Pussycat?" He said, "How the hell do you sing like that?"

Does it annoy you when people come up and sing "What's New, Pussycat?" in your face?

No. It's a compliment. As long as they're not making fun of it.

Like Elvis, you appeal to both men and women, but there are more women in the audience.

There are a lot of men there, which sometimes is over-looked. Reading some reviews you'd think there were only middle-aged women. But it's not true. Maybe they are more vocal. I get a lot of mail from men.

Describe your strangest fan letter.

There's one woman in San Francisco. She says she's had sex with everybody. She tells me about her daily routine and how she's still longing for the day when we can be together, which is going to happen *very soon.*

What did it do to your ego when you first realized the babes were hot for you?

It was wonderful! The only thing was, you had to be careful of their boyfriends. And husbands. I've had bottles thrown at me.

There have been times when your career was out of sync with trends of the minute.

That's right. As the years went on, kids kept coming up to me and saying, "Why don't you record the stuff we see you singing onstage?" But I couldn't get a record company to look at me. Until I recorded Prince's song, "Kiss."

How did people treat you when you were out of the limelight?

If you're not getting hit records, people wonder why. They say, "What happened?" and there's no answer. The songs aren't coming your way, you aren't getting the hits, and you're not on TV. You just wait to hear, "Oh, wow, there he is again."

I love the version of "Unbelievable" you did with Sandra Bernhard on TV, especially the part where you're singing to her and she gets down on the floor like she wants you to mount her.

She is nuts! In rehearsal she didn't do *any* of that.

What do you say to a woman who has her legs spread apart and a microphone between them?

I just looked at her like, "What are you doing on your knees?"

You used to wear really tight pants. Did they ever split onstage?

A number of times. I was wearing a leather outfit when I was doing a TV special in Wales [in 87] and I was doing a squat. And they split up the back. Thank God I was wearing red underwear, because sometimes I just wear a jockstrap. I bent over, turned to the camera, and said, "For those people who think I don't wear underwear." Then for the "Kiss" video I bought a new black suit. The same thing happened. I don't wear tight pants now.

What kind of underwear do you wear?

Marks and Spencer.

Are you sick of all the panty questions that you've been asked over the years?

It just gets in the way. Twenty years ago, ladies throwing underwear was a new thing. But everyone focused on that more than my talent!

Did you ever get hit in the face with a pair?

Oh, sure. I would pick them up and say, "Whose are these? What size are they?"

Do you still get panties thrown at you?

It happens, but I don't make anything out of it. The biggest problem is if a woman comes up in front and stands there dangling it. It's distracting.

How did all of this get started?

At the Copacabana in New York in 1968. At the time there was no stage. The performer sang on the floor, and the more popular you were, the closer everything would get. One night I was there singing, and some lady hands me a napkin to wipe the sweat off of my face. And then this other woman gives me her underwear. Earl Wilson, the gossip columnist, was there, saw it, and put it in his column the following day. And then they were coming at me from all directions. At the time it was fun. But you become a bloody caricature of yourself.

When you look at a woman, what is the first thing you look at?

It all depends how close I am. If it's from a distance, it's an overall thing. If I'm close, it's the eyes; it has a lot to do with the eyes.

What's the hardest thing about being a sex symbol?

Keeping in shape.

What is it about you that makes you sexy?

The performance. I've got a good bone structure. I've got a little too much of it at the moment, but my frame is good.

What do you think of plastic surgery? Have you had any?

It all depends how far you go with it. You see some people and they have it all pulled flat as a pancake. I had a broken nose so I had it fixed. My eyelids were getting a little too heavy, so they pulled a little skin out of 'em.

Who's older, you or Mick Jagger?

I'm fifty-three. He'll be fifty in July.

You've been married for over thirty years. What's the secret?

The love you have for each other has to be stronger than separation. You have to feel, What's the good of splitting up? We're always thinking about each other. When you really love one another, you become part of one another.

Is it the meat or the motion?

If you don't have the meat, then the motion is no good. It's not what you do, it's the way you do it. You have to have both.

Have you ever had an erection onstage?

No, I'm too busy singing. When you're concentrating you're just not thinking about it.

What's better, sex or performing?

It's close. Performing lasts longer.

What advice would you give to a young man who wants to seduce a woman?

Try a little tenderness.

Russ Meyer
Tempest in a D Cup

Russ Meyer is a man with an obsession, a man with a one-track mind—breasts. Big breasts. *Huge breasts.* He is the consummate tit man, and has built a filmmaking career that has spanned three decades of "gravity-defying, bra-busting boobs." As one of the most successful independent filmmakers in Hollywood, he directs, produces, writes, edits, and even distributes his own movies, which star those "super busty, double-D buxom beauties."

Meyer's films have achieved a cult status, especially for viewers in their twenties and thirties, who reached puberty when he was at the height of his moviemaking, beginning in 1969 and continuing into the 70s.

His classic film *Faster Pussycat! Kill! Kill!* was described by John Waters as "the best movie ever made" and it became the model for the characters in Waters' own films—especially Divine. ("The one big difference," says Waters, "was that Divine was a man and his big set of knockers was nothing but a pile of old washrags.")

I decided to visit the sixty-six-year-old filmmaker at his home nestled high in the lush Hollywood Hills. As I walked through his frontyard I could clearly see the "Hollywood" sign. Before I knocked on the door I thought to myself, Maybe this guy will be a real perv, a dirty old man with a raincoat who will open the door and flash his weenie. Instead I found a regular guy, a nice man who likes big tits. He greeted me with a warm, fleshy handshake and invited me in. His house is red, shaped like a triangle and looks like a Swiss chalet.

"I bought the place in the late seventies," he told me, "I bought it to shoot *Ultravixens* because it had high ceilings, so I could get up there and shoot. When we first started shooting, we had so much junk in the backyard that the neighbors complained it looked like Tijuana."

I sat down on his large, brown Naugahyde couch. Big breasts were everywhere; so were framed posters from all of his movies, reviews, clippings, and memorabilia, covering every inch from floor to ceiling.

"You really love breasts," I said.

"They're an obsession," he said, directing his responses to my cleavage.

"This place is like a museum," I said.

"It's a shrine," he said.

A shrine to giant tits.

"Have a look around," he said, waving his arms.

I looked around. I spotted a pair of tittie mugs with big pink nipples on the shelf, then looked at some photos of his well-endowed stars.

"Breasts are comforting," he said. "They're fulfilling, giving, warm, fun."

I looked up and felt the warmth.

"Where did you dig up these busty actresses?" I asked.

"They're mostly strippers," he told me. "Kitten [Natividad, one of his 'biggest' stars, with whom he lived for five years] found them for me. She would find one and say, 'Wait till you see her tits!' You know, one big-breasted woman usually attracts another."

Meyer looks like Ernie Kovacs, with a mustache, pointed eyebrows, and a mischievous gleam in his eye. He is soft-spoken and actually has a sexy voice. He seems like a man who has enjoyed his life to the fullest, literally.

I told him that girls in their twenties like his movies because the women are strong, aggressive, more like women of the 90s.

"The women are the driving force in my films," he said. "I like women who are aggressive. And stacked. It's always been my thing. I like a woman who comes on like the Santa Fe Super Chief. I think women are the superior beings. I like women who are archetypes, women who are *beyond* women. It's been my taste throughout my lifetime. The men in my movies are sufficiently muscular and klutzy."

His tried-and-true formula is, in a word, "Bosommania," or as he describes it, "outrageously buxom women and dumb, muscular men laying their sexually aggressive prowess on the line." It seems to have worked, with thirteen out of his twenty-two titles available and as popular as ever on the videocassette markets.

Foreigners are also attracted to his films. "The Dutch are real tit men, I'll tell you. And the Germans and the English. My films are satires. I've always done things because they were enormously appealing to me. [Meyer's conversation is permeated with superlatives like *enormous, monumental, big.*] My films should be laugh-provoking, ridiculous. The narrators are like the ones in *The March of Time.* But they're narrating about somebody getting laid! And then it's juiced up by the music; a big band, a thirty-seven-piece orchestra. Very stirring. And then you have two people pawing at each other in the woods."

Meyer began his career as a combat cameraman during World War II. After the war, he made industrial films and then started shooting girls for pinup magazines. "I started to shoot every lady I knew," he said. "It was a big turn-on!" Then he shot his second wife, Eve, for one of the early centerfolds in *Playboy.* In 1959 he made his first movie, *The Immortal Mr. Teas,* featuring his interest in "female pulchritude," as well as voyeurism, the girl next door, and peeping Toms. Most of his films were made on shoestring budgets, and all but three made money theatrically. (The three, *Blacksnake*, *Up*, and *Ultravixens* are now showing a profit as video releases.) *Mr. Teas* was made with $24,000 and grossed over a million. *Supervixens* was made for $219,000 and grossed over $17 million, making Meyer comfortable for life. Other movies, like *Mondo Topless*, featuring eight "buxotic" women jiggling their hooters, were big hits at drive-ins when the topless craze hit in the 60s.

In 1969, his film *Vixen* was the second movie to be rated X. "The first," he said, "was a film starring Marianne Faithfull called *Girl on a Motorcycle*. Warner Bros. was so shocked it got an X that they put it away and hid it." Roger Ebert, who wrote the screenplay for Meyer's *Beyond the Valley of the Dolls*, constantly defends him from accusations that he's a pornographer. "When I say my movies are rated an MPAA 'X,' " says Meyer, "I mean they are soft-core. I hate that word, but they are not the hard-core X, the purple X. I am not interested in hard-core pornography. It's not humorous."

"How did you meet Roger Ebert?" I asked.

"He has a taste that I share," he said. "Tits. That's it. That's how we met. He is a firm believer in what I do. Our relationship goes beyond tits, though. Whether it's fishing or having a little fun in a swimming pool with a couple of girls . . ."

"How would you describe your book?" I asked.

"The book is like a movie in a sense. I talk about over twenty women who were very close to me. There's nothing negative about this book. It's all happy, fun. I write in a buoyant style.

And there is a six-page foreword by Roger. There's some rough verbiage in it. The language is strong—Jackie Collins will want to crawl under a rock after she reads it. I have so many words for breasts that you won't believe it! [e.g. jungle drums]. The descriptions of women are monumental. I think there will be a great interest in the parts about my sexual exploits. It was done with great presentation and pleasure. And the noises! Aaaaaaaarrrrrrhhh!" he growls. "Hummingbirds, toggle bolts, the edge of wetness . . ."

Next, Meyer (who, by this time, I was calling Russ) gave me a tour of the rest of his house, including the cutting room, distribution center, and offices of RM Films International, Inc. In the kitchen, wooden plaques were mounted with mementos from each of his films. On one plaque, I noticed a blue diaphragm case. "Whose is this?" I asked. "That one was Kitten's from *Beneath the Valley of the Ultravixens*. Its a size sixty!" On another plaque was his first handheld camera and on a third a broken heel and hotel keys. The one that caught my attention had two cups, one inscribed with "Russ loves Kitten" and the other with "I Love Russ." Beneath the two cups was a chewed-up douche bag. "That was Kitten's," he pointed out.

After the tour Russ invited me out to dinner with George, his editor, and Stan, RM's distributor in England. "He's a proper Englishman," Russ told me. Why would he want to go out with us? I wondered. Then I thought that maybe he was the repressed type who washes his hands every five minutes but is really kinky. In any case, we all jumped into Meyer's big white recreational vehicle, the kind that seats a crowd. We went to a restaurant with brown leather chairs like the ones in Russ's house and sat in an area roped off by a sign reading "The Playpen," a sign Russ seemed to be comfortable with.

After we all downed a couple of drinks, the conversation became even more sexual than it had been.

"Were you aroused when you were shooting your movies?" I asked.

"I had a hard-on the whole time," he said. "It's what gave my films that edge, that *quality*. It was good to be hungry. Everything I did was a turn-on."

I asked him what he thought of women who have their breasts reduced. He scoffed at the question, shaking his head in disgust.

"A lot of the women I know had them enlarged," he said.

I looked down at my own breasts, breasts that had always seemed just the right size. But suddenly, sitting next to Russ Meyer, I wasn't so sure. "You like girls who have at least a D cup, right?" I said. "I'm not sure if I'm big enough to be in one of your movies. But, you know, Russ, just sitting next to you, I think they're getting bigger."

"Yeah," he said, laughing, "they're swelling right up."

"What do you think of women who are flat?" I asked.

He looked perplexed for a moment, as if the word *flat* did not exist in his vocabulary.

"I'd rather be playing cards," he said.

"The women in your movies are the kind of women I would think some men wished their women would be more like," I said. "They're wild."

"I like women who are always in heat," he said. "There aren't enough of those women to go around."

At this point, the two tequilas must have gone to my head because I started to babble. "Don't you think women are sexy because they think about sex a lot?" George and Stan nodded their heads in agreement. "And don't you think that people who are unsexy never think about sex?" I said, thinking I was being psychologically probing. Then I asked Russ what he thinks makes a women sexy.

"Big tits," he answered.

After dinner, we drove back up the winding road toward the hills, past a small restaurant where, Russ tells us, Kitten, on their first date, got so bombed that when she went to the bathroom she got her zipper caught in her "pubicity." Then our conversation turned to why it's so exciting to have sex in a strange hotel room. "I always want to check in under an assumed name," said Russ.

Back at his house, Russ ran upstairs, then came down and gave me four of his movies, a kiss on the cheek, and a big hug, making sure that my 36C's rubbed against his chest.

John Waters
Flamingos' Rogue at Home

A man who has grossed out millions, earned the title "The Prince of Puke," and been arrested for indecent exposure is a man I would seriously consider as a marriage partner. John Waters says he is a "negative role model for a new generation of bored youths," which is why I wanted to meet him.

Waters made his first movie, a short called *Hag in a Black Leather Jacket*, in 1964. *Roman Candles*, in 1966, marked the debut of Divine, whose image Waters helped to create. His first feature, *Mondo Trasho*, was completed in 1969. During filming he and two actors were arrested for indecent exposure. *Multiple Maniacs* was next, made for an audience, according to Waters, "frantically searching for a film more hideous and unreal than any previously seen." *Pink Flamingos*, his most widely known film, premiered in 1972. It was billed as an "exercise in poor taste" and earned the title "one of the sickest movies ever made." The plot revolves around two groups of social outcasts vying for the title of "the filthiest people alive." The movie contains Waters's most remembered scenes: the party where someone's asshole covers the screen and dances to wild 50s music and the "happy ending" where Divine eats a freshly laid dog turd.

Female Trouble (1974) tells a criminal's life story from teenage brathood to electrocution and features Divine giving birth on the couch in a leopard print dress and heels. *Desperate Living* introduced Jean Hill, a 400-pound maid who squashes her employer to death by sitting on his face. *Polyester*, released in 1981, was filmed in "odorama"; with audience participation scratch-and-sniff cards featuring the fragrances of stinky tennis shoes and Tab Hunter's flatulence. This was followed by *Hairspray* in 1988 and *Cry-Baby* starring Johnny Depp, in 1990. *Serial Mom*, his twelfth film, stars Kathleen Turner, as a "normal" suburban housewife who kills people who are mean to her children or husband.

Waters continues to live in Baltimore, Hairdo Capital of the World. I drove down with my brother and father. Once in Waters's neighborhood, we passed nothing but beauty parlors and liquor stores. My father, who suddenly looked perplexed, asked, "Why do you want to interview such a weirdo?" My brother and I shared an aberrant glance. Finally we found the right house. My father dropped us off and drove away.

John Waters opened the door and greeted us with a crooked smile. He looked like a cross between a white Little Richard, a creepy Don Knotts, and a lingerie sales-man. Behind him, in the hallway, was an authentic-looking electric chair. "Oh, that," he says. "That was Divine's in *Female Trouble*. I decorate it instead of a Christmas tree."

Visiting John Waters's apartment is like ending up at a guy's place on the first date and realizing that he is strange and you might want to get out fast. Actually, it looks like a spacious Upper West Side apartment. It's deceptively nor-mal, almost old-fashioned—like Grandma's. Until you start noticing the details. Pieces of plastic meat and boxes of fake chocolate sit on a table in the living room. Above the fireplace is a frightening framed oil painting of Gertrude Baniazeweski, a serial killer. "She was only thirty at the time of the portrait," Waters giggles, "but I told the painter to make her look more like forty, and uglier."

In the bedroom I meet Waters's "roommates": Tina, Kathy, and Kim, you-do-the-hair-dolls with bouffants and black liquid eyeliner that he makes them wear. "They don't get out much," he says. "I took them with me for the first time on my last trip. I was hoping that the X-ray man at the airport wouldn't ask to look inside my suitcase."

We move to the den, past the photos of a young Liberace and Patty McCormack, the little girl who pushed people in wheelchairs down stairwells and killed anyone who crossed her in *The Bad Seed*. On the shelves are hundreds of books, including *Jules and Jim Jones, Co-Ed Killers*, and *Good Girls Gone Bad*. On the opposite wall is a certificate from Patuxent prison, where Waters taught filmmaking, listing each prisoner's crime and time ("John Smith, rape/assault with a deadly weapon/thirty years"). The other walls are covered with posters for his films in French and Italian, along with some for Russ Meyer's and other exploitation and horror movies.

"Please don't reveal my exact address," Waters begs as we sit down. Overenthusiastic fans like to send him bowel movements in the mail. "Opening the mail has become a dreaded event," he confides. "At a screening once, two groupies appalled me by saying, 'Wow, that last scene where Divine eats shit really turned my lover and me on. Now we eat each other's shit all the time!' I knew my films attracted weirdos, but this was one minority I hadn't counted on."

As Waters politely serves us tea, I wonder what shocks him. "I think people who consider themselves normal are the most bizarre," he says. "I like real things that something is the matter with, that's what I'm interested in. If someone or something is always bizarre, there is no irony. You need contrast. Every person has something weird about him. Try to imagine every person and what their hidden thing is. Every neighbor interviewed about a mass killer always says he was a really nice guy. Two brothers can have the same upbringing, one kills thirty people, the other is a brain surgeon. There's no answer to that and that's why I'm still interested—it's one of my obsessions. Ten years later *Pink Flamingos* shocks *me*. That artificial insemination scene is really ugly. I mean, I'm proud of that film, but I don't want to do it again. I did it at an age when it was good to have rage. But I don't think it's good to have rage at age forty-six. It would be like having a mohawk. When you see a forty-six-year-old with a mohawk, he looks like a big idiot."

Hairspray, which takes place in Baltimore in 1962, relives a time Waters remembers well. "It was the height of the beehive period, when Kennedy was in office and hippies hadn't appeared yet. I wanted to make a satire of this period because it was such a ludicrous look. Of course, it's exaggerated—Debbie Harry's hair goes up to the ceiling, and nobody had hair that high. It was a time where everyone worked hard on their look, sort of like today. And a time of no sex. Sort of like today."

We talk about what makes people think something is in "bad taste," and he says, "There is such a thing as good bad taste and bad bad taste. Good bad taste can be creatively nauseating, but at the same time appeals to the especially twisted sense of humor, which is anything but universal."

Speaking of bad taste, I ask Waters why he has cast such actors as Sonny Bono and Pia Zadora.

"They're my idea of movie stars," he answers. "They're originals. No one says, 'Go out and get me a Sonny Bono type.' I first saw Pia in a trailer for the film *Butterfly* and liked her jailbait appeal.

"If I have a casting gimmick in *Serial Mom*, it's that I was going for A-list actors . . . people who you wouldn't expect to see in a John Waters film because they're associated with serious work. The first time I saw Kathleen Turner in the scene where she's running down the street with a butcher knife in her hand, it was like a dream come true. I felt like I was in cinema heaven. She is the Breck Girl gone crazy.

"I'm always fascinated by people's secret lives," he continues. "And I believe everyone has one. I can go into a McDonald's up the street and watch families . . . and I wonder if she likes her mother, and what her mother did to her. I wonder if a couple's sex life is good, and if their children like them.

"*Hairspray* is rated PG. I think it's hilarious that a whole family can come and see that movie. It's like a real sneak attack. The censor board can't come and hassle me and tell me I can't show this. But my sensibility is still there. *Polyester* looked down in a sort of snotty way at the characters. *Hairspray* has more of a fondness for them.

"*Serial Mom* is a comedy about a subject that is normally considered anything but humorous—serial killers and mass murderers. I've always thought it very interesting that you can take a topic that is generally considered quite tragic and magically put it on a movie screen, and all of a sudden it has the potential to be funny."

For years, Waters has followed major criminal trials and is always amused to see how killers become instant media celebrities. "Now as soon as you commit a crime, the agents are there and you're on TV the next week," he says.

Serial Mom was filmed in the suburbs of Baltimore, close to the neighborhood where Waters attended private grade school, public junior high school, and a Catholic high school for boys. He recalls that suburbia "was one of the first places I fled from, which makes it an even stranger place to come back to.

"The city of Baltimore has always had its own eccentric version of things, that's why I still live here. The part of Baltimore that inspires me will never change. It's the kind of place where you can still see sleazy strip bars, grandmothers with tattoos, and lots of great hairdos. It's a polyester town, hairspray land. And it will always obsess me. And to become a successful artist, you have to be totally obsessed."

Antonio Banderas
Spain's Mucho Movie Star

Madonna said you were the sexiest guy in the world in *Truth or Dare*. What do you think of her?

I think she's courageous. She's always looking to break barriers. In a way, she's in a difficult position. Maybe it's too high, but she defends it well. She's tough. I like that. I'm grateful to her for those three minutes of publicity she gave me. It was better exposure than a paid advertisement.

Were you a playboy before you met your wife?

No. To be a playboy you have to be very secure, and I'm very insecure.

Why?

Because I have doubts about myself professionally. Sometimes it's good to be insecure. When you are successful in this field and thinking of the moon and stars, you can get lost. You have to come down eventually. This insecurity keeps me from flying too high.

What is your formula for seduction?

Improvisation.

In *Law of Desire* and *Philadelphia* you played gay characters. As a hetero, was it difficult to prepare for those gay love scenes?

In *Law of Desire*, we just laughed a lot after we had to kiss each other. You know, it's strange: people are willing to accept murders on the screen, but they can't deal with two men kissing.

How did you start acting in films?

I had been working in Madrid at the National Theater for five years when Pedro Almodóvar came to the theater and saw the play. He came into the dressing room and asked, "Do you want to make a movie with me?" That's how it began. I continued working with him, acting in *Labyrinth of Passion, Matador, Law of Desire*, and *Tie Me Up! Tie Me Down!* Almodóvar was my passport to the U.S. I left [Spain] with a little pain in my heart when I came to Hollywood to make *The Mambo Kings*.

Your character in that film is rather a sad fellow.

Nestor has a lot of problems. He's an artist, but he has difficulty communicating with the world. He needs his trumpet and his music to save himself. He's always sick when it comes to love. The result is a very romantic, melancholy film. He comes to New York from Cuba with his brother in the 50s, but he never forgets his first love, Maria. She begins to represent an idea, maybe Cuba. The things he likes best are those he can't have.

Quién es más macho, Fernando Lamas o Ricky Ricardo?

Those are the two most important Latin guys in the U.S., no? It was unbelievable, the similarity between Desi Arnaz, Jr., and his father, who he plays in the movie. We appeared on the "I Love Lucy" show performing at the Tropicana. Everything was supposed to look like it did in the 50s. It was fun for me but I think it was very emotional for him.

What were you like as a child? Was your family eccentric? Did you get into much trouble?

I was very timid and always restless. Maybe I chose acting as a form of therapy, as a way to enable myself to communicate to the rest of the world. My family was very normal. My father worked in the state department, my mother was a teacher, my brother an economist.

You are perhaps the most famous young actor in Spain. What's the worst thing about fame?

In general, fame is a condition where people recognize you walking on the street. To be recognized for being famous is one thing, ultimately not very significant. To be recognized for your work is much more satisfying.

What did you like about making Hollywood films?

This whole country is a movie, a wild Technicolor dream. It's not unlike an Almodóvar set.

In *Tie Me Up! Tie Me Down!* you tied up your costar. Was that the first time you ever pulled out the ropes?

Yes, but it wasn't the last.

Are you a day person or a night person?

I like morning. Sunday morning is my favorite. Nothing to do but lie in bed. Every morning should be Sunday morning.

Do you play any sports?

I play soccer. But it's difficult to do so often because you have to call twenty-one other guys to play. I don't have that many friends.

What is it that makes a woman sexy?

I like a woman with long, long legs and a short, short skirt.

Did you ever get a hard-on doing love scenes?

Generally, no. Sometimes it takes six hours to film one scene. It's difficult to keep an erection for that long.

Fred Schneider
Minor Pop Star/Major Goofball

Was it fun doing a remake of "The Flintstone's" theme song?
They let us do it our way.

Who are your favorite characters in "The Flintstones"?
Snagglepuss and Dino.

How did you start your career?
I used to get tipsy on those Polynesian cocktails with little umbrellas and make up songs with my friends on the toy piano and walkie-talkie.

Did you ever take voice lessons?
When I first started singing, I had to fake it. My voice was really off-key. Then I took some singing lessons. Now my voice is so good I'm ready to get involved in dinner theater!

The B52's have been called a "party band"...
I like to whoop it up for the people I perform for. I guess it comes from my experience at parties. I can start a conga line at the drop of a hat.

You get a hit record, a Grammy nomination, a Radio City Music gig, and a Letterman appearance. Then what happens?
Everybody wants to be your friend.

What's the best thing someone yelled to you on the street?
"Hey, Love Shack Man!" I liked that.

What's different about performing on stage and on TV?
I always hate the unflattering camera angles that make me look like I have three chins when I really have only two.

Do you have any teenage groupies?
Nah, I'm too weird-looking.

I think you're cute. Maybe you should consider becoming a supermodel.

Well I am available for supermodeling any time. I went to the Divine school of modeling.

You have offbeat beauty. Sandra Bernhard is signed up with Ford. And Debi Mazar is signed up with Flick.

Maybe I'll sign up with Hick.

What kind of fan mail do you get?

One sixteen-year-old girl said she wanted me to be her dad. That made me feel really old.

Have you ever lied about your age?

Oh, yes, everyone should. It's good to confuse people. They always think you're older or younger anyway. I tell people I'm seventy and they tell me I look great.

Do you think everyone over thirty should go to the gym?

Yes, it's embarrassing when it's dragging on the floor.

What sexercises do you do?

The old up and down. It's good for the biceps.

What do you think is sexy?

Nude volleyball.

Have you ever had bad sex?

Everybody's had that.

Where's a good place to have sex?

On the front lawn of an abandoned building.

If you were offered a role in a movie, would you perform a nude scene?

Yes, especially if it was a major feature film and nudity was essential to the plot.

Is it the meat or the motion?

It's the *e*motion.

What are your turn-offs?

Anyone with limburgy, garlicy breath and anyone with a "good" personality.

What's more important, looks or personality?

These days it's looks.

Who is your favorite fashion designer?

Pat Perkins—she designed the clothes for "The Honeymooners." And whoever designed the clothes for "The Jetsons."

What is your fashion philosophy?

I like setting trends, then abandoning them when everyone else adopts them.

You wrote a song about having a monster in your pants.

It was about a dinosaur who always wore the same polka-dot pants.

What do you think is a good look?

I like the "wing ding" look. You know, totally mismatched plaids and dots, polyester ensembles that look truly awful.

Do you think the Pope has ever played with himself?

I'm sure. I bet there's a whole love thing going on over at the Vatican.

What did you read as a kid?

Mad magazine and comic books.

What will life be in 2094?

They'll have found ways to keep everyone alive, but we'll all look dreadful!

I need your advice. People always ask me what kind of parents I have. They look disappointed when I tell them that my parents are wonderful and normal. What should I tell them?

Tell them your parents are swingers.

Joeseph Pluchino

Appendix

Male Bonding

Answering My Men of Letters

Each time the mailman approaches, I anxiously wait to see his package. From the poetic to the pathetic, letters from my readers always delight and excite me. Apparently, it's a thrill for them too; as one enthusiastic reader put it: "I can't help it. I'm beating my meat with one hand and writing with the other."

My letters arrive from across the country, as well as from Canada, Germany, and from soldiers who say they're bored in Somalia. Some are addressed from work, written by people who are busy "looking busy." Others are written at 3:00 in the morning and include descriptions of the writers as "undersexed," or "not real kinky but a toe sucker." Some end their letters with "Your dream lover," "Your future date," or "Yours in desperation."

The tone ranges from the critical ("You hurt the male ego") to the complimentary ("What I respect is your honesty and, well, your large breasts"). A few are fanatical and say things like "I want to pay tribute to you and name my band 'Anka.'" Some offer unsolicited opinions of me, like the self-described "twenty-year-old whiteboy" who thinks I am "open-minded." He writes, "As I read your words lying on the sofa, I find myself oblivious to my mom's insane nagging to do the dishes." One college student presumed I was "really out to party and hang out." A thirty-year-old Air Force pilot called me "Camille Paglia on Ecstasy."

Most letters have the ulterior motive of asking me out. Their overtures are flattering, but I question their intentions when they write statements like "I am easy to get along with. I have never hit my girlfriends. Come to think of it, none of them have ever hit me either. But I have tied some up and spanked them after they expressed a desire for that form of affection."

Sometimes I wish men in real life would say some of the things they say to me anonymously through the mail. One said, "You sound like an amazing, romantic woman." Another said, "I would do anything to go out with you." Some men have even offered to buy me plane tickets to visit them or have asked to whisk me away to some paradise island. This is a switch, considering I live in New York and the last two boyfriends I had were too cheap to buy me beers.

Some of the more romantic letters map out our dream date.

One guy said, "We would embrace each other by the fire, hold on tight, and never let go." This sounded wonderful, but unfortunately he didn't enclose a photo. I hate to be superficial, but the last time I accepted a date with a guy I never saw, it was through a personal ad. He described himself as looking like "a young Cary Grant." When I met him he looked more like Walter Matthau and walked with a limp and a cane.

Like Brigitte Nielson, who met Sylvester Stallone by sending him a provocative photo of herself, men who enclose their photos have the best chance of becoming my pen pals. One guy, however, made the mistake of sending in a beaming photo of himself standing next to Dan Quayle. Another sent in a photo of himself on a wine brochure. A few sent in acting headshots. One guy was creative and sent in a photo of himself with his arm around an ex-girlfriend. He cut her out of the picture and in the empty space penciled in "Vacant." A number of men sent in photos taken with their sisters or children. This was fine, and shows they are family men, but I draw the line at men who send in photos with their wives.

In addition to photos, I also receive multimedia gifts. One guy, who sold condoms at Lallapaloosa, sent me about fifty. Maybe he hopes that every time I use one I will think of him. One aspiring filmmaker sent a videotape of himself (a good idea), while another sports enthusiast sent his used jockstrap (a bad idea; I instantly threw it out the window, it caught on a tree, and I've had to watch it deteriorate ever since). One poet from San Francisco sent me a cassette tape of his poems, with a photo invitation to one of his readings. His get-up consisted of a black lacy teddy with no underwear and a visible penis. (It looked like he had a half-chub.) The tape was enticingly titled "Cleaning the Vomit Out of Her Car." His accompanying letter ended with "I hope my work will make you feel like taking a shower." I listened to the tape and actually liked his poetry because it was so neo-Beat. My favorite line was "The mucus hung from my nostrils like cheese from a slice of pizza." His poems seemed to focus on boogers, mucus, vomit, salty wounds, and other bodily fluids. After this, I not only wanted to take a shower, but I needed to be fumigated.

Because I open my bedroom window to write openly about sexuality, many correspondents mistakenly think they have a view into my brain. They think I will enjoy their sexually explicit letters. I don't. Especially when they fall into the "psycho/porno" category. One guy writing on Garfield stationery started out sounding normal. "I just read your article about breaking up with your boyfriend. I hope you get over any pain you may have felt and hope you find someone compatible." Then the letter got worse: "Your article on aphrodisiacs was an aphrodisiac in itself." Next the letter became abusive: "I naturally produce lots of sperm and it is snow white, thick, and super-yummy tasting. Some day I hope to cover your face with it." He ended with a schizoid romantic flourish: "If you would like to be my pen pal, I would be delighted to hear from you. You would love the way my hog looks." Fortunately, most of the creepier mail ends with "Unfortunately, I am unable to visit New York due to circumstances beyond my control."

One eager reader wrote in asking if he could be my assistant. "I would like to work for you," he said, offering to help me with "typing or product research." A list of his credentials followed:

"I speak three languages and have an innocent, preppylike appearance which allows me to be three times as perverted. Enclosed is a list of foreign synonyms for penis and vagina (*pennosh, boxina, zwenish, yuanyainya*). I am also an expert on anuses, if I may take the liberty to boast." I sent his résumé to the Condé Nast personnel department.

Since *Details* is a men's magazine, only about 15 percent of my mail comes from women. One, who said she stole her boyfriend's copy, told me, "Thanks for advising men on what women like. Your article on cunnilingus was enthusiastically received." Another said all the women in her office read the article about male prostitutes and wanted to know where they could order the "hot Italian sausage" I mentioned. A third sent me my first mail-in lesbian proposal. She is a Yugoslavian-born woman who related to the sound of my name and the subject of prostitution. "I run the first gay women's escort service in London," she wrote. And because I mentioned that I spent $900 researching the piece, she invited me to come stay with her for free.

In addition to love letters, I also receive hate mail. Fortunately, this arrives in small amounts. One guy expressed his opinion that I represent "smug, narcissistic, and pretentious women all over the world." A second liked the first piece he read, but by the third, changed his opinion. His letter grew angrier as it went on: "I've lived the life of a cockroach for seven years struggling to become a writer. I got pissed off when I saw you 'selling out.' " He told me to change my style of writing and added, "Change your name if need be." Because of his advice I have decided to change my name to 🐛 following

Prince's example. Another irate reader was furious about a statement where I mentioned that size really doesn't matter, but that some women do admit to liking a big one. He wrote: "I've always been self-conscious about the size of my penis, and your article made me feel like shit."

On the innocent side was a letter from Matt, written in several colors of Crayola. He crayoned, "You see, I've assumed by reading, contemplating, and through dream analysis that you're having trouble finding 'the perfect guy.' I'm not him or anything, but going out with me, I bet you could figure out everything you *don't* want. I'm not old enough to drink yet, so I can't go to clubs without my mom. Anyway, my main interests are skateboarding, snowboarding, and talking loudly about masturbation and my penis in public." This obsession with their organs is common among my readers. They also share a tendency toward chronic masturbation.

Although I receive about a hundred letters each month, the rate varies according to the topics I am writing about. The piece that prompted the most response was the one on personal ads. Suddenly, dozens of letters streamed in, written in the form of personal ads. The writers described everything from their musical tastes ("I like Nine Inch Nails and Neil Diamond") to their physical attributes ("I have a well-developed love muscle"). One guy wrote, "Come to Seattle where the men are sensitive and strong and dance naked in the rain." This sounded appealing until he added, "Ted Bundy was from here."

After my two-month run as the Determinator, curious readers began asking me for advice. One guy wrote, "I have a large birthmark on my penis and I want to know if I should cover it with a tattoo." (Try a Band-Aid.) Another said, "I am in love with a girl who has no interest in sleeping with me. I want to ask her to get married. What should I do?" (Never marry anyone who won't sleep with you, unless you want to join the millions of married men who also have that problem.)

One letter responded to a sentence I wrote in the sex survey article about the number of eighteen- to twenty-one-year-old virgins. The letter, written by two students at Georgetown University, said, "We are both eighteen and virgins. We were so excited when we read your sex survey article where you mentioned that maybe you should 'start visiting college campuses, scouting for boys willing to learn.' Let us tell you that there are no boys more willing to learn than us and we don't think there could be a better instructor than you. We would be in heaven if you could come to Georgetown to teach us about making love and pleasing a woman. You are looking at the greatest turn-on in your life." For a second, I considered this offer from an erotic/teenage love slave standpoint. But then I visualized the scenario and imagined two bumbling, fumbling freshman fighting over who goes first. Then I flashed back to what sex was like at eighteen—and how bad it was.

The most painstakingly written letters come from my largest constituency of fans—federal prisoners. Now here's a demographic I always hoped for: a bunch of guys with lots of time on their hands and hands in their pants a lot of the time. Their letters are often at least four pages long, are usually very polite, and always strive for neat penmanship, and for some reason the men fill every line on the paper, including the margins. These letters always include descriptions of themselves ("I have a bald, hairless style, my eyes are hazel, and I can see for miles and miles"), and their times and crimes ("I've been in prison since I was sixteen and have been without a female person for eight years").

Because prisoners crave contact, jail mail tends to be more manipulative. Prisoners say things like, "Don't let the fact that I am in prison dissuade you from starting a relationship with me." (As if I see myself going to the prison to make conjugal visits in a trailer.) Some say things like, "I am writing in purple because it carries strong vibrations," or "I want you to be my pen friend" or "my lady." One said, "I want to push all your mental, physical, and spiritual buttons." Another said, "Woman, I would caress you with my mouth and make you pray." And everyone promises, "It will all be different when I'm out." (That's when I'll sign up for the witness protection program.)

Since prisoners have extra "leisure" hours, this gives them time to express their views in writing. One inmate, Frank, suggested that "women should behave more like Anka" and told me to look him up when he's "out in 94." His letter was subsequently printed on the Letters to the Editor page. Three weeks later I received a note from a fellow inmate of Frank's. He had a crush on Frank and was crushed to learn that Frank had a crush on me. (Crushes always work that way.) Suddenly I was involved in a dramatic love triangle. When he finally got over his crush he wrote again to say that, of all the girls in the world he would like to see Frank with, it would be me.

That letter was one of my favorites. To any future correspondents, I offer these few suggestions: Do be sincere. Do be original. Don't complain about how miserable your sex life is. I'm a romantic at heart, but don't send in poetry written by someone else and signed with your name. Don't drool on the paper. Don't detail the ways you would defile me. And whatever you do, don't brag about your hog.